Praise for *The Coffee Mom's Devotional*

The Coffee Mom's Devotional is like a latte full of love, with touching stories, moments of laughter, and biblical insights that will warm your heart and soul.

Trish Berg
Coffee drinker, mother of four and author of *Rattled—Surviving Your Baby's First Year without Losing Your Cool* and *The Great American Supper Swap*

This is a book that meets us in the gut-checking moments of life, but it doesn't leave us there. Instead it challenges us toward balance, toward realism and, most of all, toward a deeper relationship with God. So order yourself a double caramel mocha and read on!

Julie-Allyson Ieron
Conference speaker and author of *Praying Like Jesus* and *An Overwhelmed Woman's Guide to . . . Caring for Aging Parents*

In her disarmingly conversational style, Celeste Palermo serves up a delightful blend of humor, wit, life experience and practical insights, all grounded in biblical truth. Get it for the moms in your life, but don't be afraid to have a soul-stirring drink yourself.

Steve Moore
President and CEO, The Mission Exchange

Palermo has created a book that will inspire women young and old. Reading *The Coffee Mom's Devotional* makes me wish I could put on a big pair of fuzzy slippers and old pajamas, and go have popcorn and soda with her on her couch.

Sarah Smiley
Syndicated columnist and author of *I'm Just Saying* (www.sarahsmiley.com)

I savored the insights in *The Coffee Mom's Devotional*. Some moms depend on their daily dose of caffeine to get through the day. Celeste reminds us to "drink in the fullness of God."

Beth K. Vogt
Author of *Baby Changes Everything: Embracin[g]
Motherhood after 35*

This book is dedicated to my mom,
Linda Titcomb,
who lives her life by example,
sharing wisdom
and modeling the very themes in this book.
Thank you.

THE COFFEE MOM'S DEVOTIONAL

A Rich Blend of
30 Brief and Inspiring
Devotions

CELESTE PALERMO

Regal

From Gospel Light
Ventura, California, U.S.A.

Published by Regal
From Gospel Light
Ventura, California, U.S.A.
www.regalbooks.com
Printed in the U.S.A.

Library of Congress Cataloging-in-Publication Data
Palermo, Celeste, 1972-
The coffee mom's devotional : a rich blend of 30 brief and inspiring devotions /
Celeste Palermo.
p. cm.
Includes bibliographical references.
ISBN 978-0-8307-4646-0 (trade paper)
1. Mothers—Religious life. 2. Devotional exercises. I. Title.
BV4529.18.P35 2009
242'.6431—dc22
2008039436

1 2 3 4 5 6 7 8 9 10 11 12 13 14 15 / 15 14 13 12 11 10 09

Rights for publishing this book outside the U.S.A. or in non-English languages are
administered by Gospel Light Worldwide, an international not-for-profit ministry.
For additional information, please visit www.glww.org, email info@glww.org, or write
to Gospel Light Worldwide, 1957 Eastman Avenue, Ventura, CA 93003, U.S.A.

CONTENTS

FOREWORD

My java journey began, as Celeste's did, in college, but not as a stimulant to keep me awake to study. I loved coffee ice cream. It seemed that it should be possible to replicate that taste in a cup, with the right proportion of sugar and cream—and it was! Ah, those simple pre-Starbucks days.

Now coffee is required for two of my favorite daily routines—in addition, of course, to all those random moments over coffee spent with friends. I always, always, always have two cups first thing in the morning as I review my calendar, make a list (like Celeste) for the day ahead and then (the day-planning distraction past me) give the day up to God. Coffee gets me up and going, gets me collected, gets me to ground the day with God.

The second routine is for coffee to accompany eating anything sweet: a muffin, coffee cake, a warm chocolate chip cookie. Dessert of any kind begs to be washed down with coffee. So I guess you could say coffee helps me get perspective on the day and also helps me savor the sweetness.

This is what Celeste will do in the pages ahead. She'll help you take your coffee habit (we assume you have one, dear reader) and use it as a sort of caffeinated catalyst to remind you that there is Someone larger than coffee who loves you, gives you perspective and has your circumstances in hand.

I met Celeste at a writer's conference where I was searching, on behalf of MOPS International (Mothers of Preschoolers), for exceptional writers who were in-the-trenches moms. Having spent 12 years on that search, I can tell you it isn't easy! Often moms of young children are quite naturally over-occupied with the demands of mothering, and they haven't yet gained the perspective that comes with years and that allows them to bridge from their personal experiences to provide wisdom to other moms. Celeste has a keen ability for this, as well as an exceptional gift for humor and metaphor.

You are in for a treat, whether you gulp through *The Coffee Mom's Devotional* or take it in sips. Grab a cup of your favorite coffee beverage, and see what I mean.

Mary Beth Lagerborg
Former Publishing Manager for MOPS International
Coauthor of the Bestseller *Once-a-Month Cooking*
Speaker and Author, *Dwelling: Living Fully from the Space You Call Home*

ACKNOWLEDGMENTS

My endeavors are rarely solitary. Even in my most private moments, I've usually got "help." (Moms with curious toddlers will relate.) As such, it only stands to reason that with something big—like a book—I'd have a support crew as vast as the Verizon Network. And so, with love and heartfelt gratitude, I offer a special "thank you" to:

Linda Titcomb, my editor, and more importantly, my mom. Her tireless work and wisdom have helped shape me and this book. I am so grateful.

Dan Titcomb, my dad. Thank you for your constant love and support, and for always making the coffee. You've helped provide the foundation on which I build.

Cara Maclean, my sister, who is a radiant and graceful mom to Gavin and Graeme. Thank you for finding the time to read my material and interject your priceless wit.

I deeply value the women who read my manuscript and provided honest feedback: Lori Blackwell, Monica Dukes, June Thompson, Anna Ratliff and Penny Stiffler.

The members, staff and pastors at Smoky Hill Vineyard in Centennial, Colorado, are phenomenal. There is just no other way to say it. Thank you all for walking this life of faith with me—for encouraging me and praying for me.

I am especially grateful to my senior pastor, Greg Thompson, for his guidance and friendship. My faith has truly flourished through his teaching.

Susan Holloran, Sarah Smiley, Joy Lehman, Tandi Venter, Linda Titcomb, Jane Norton, Beth Vogt, Tamy Elam and Terri Powell are the letter writers in the book. They are all moms who nourish and inspire. Thank you.

The following women are incorporated in the pages of this book—through stories, encouragement and more—a perk (or not) of being pals with a writer: Kellie Dunkirk, Jenni Weaver, Christa Jeffers, Ashley Gehrke, Heather Parrish, Carolyn Drever, Erika Wyrick,

Monica, Moira, and Georgia Dukes, Julie Hambrick, Zaira Hansson, Karen Warrington, Tandi Venter, Gretchen Flores, Coleen Ethridge, Holly Woods, Tammy Jones, Jennifer Dodd, Kim Maynes, Lori Blackwell, Lesley Barnham, Nancy Valore, Susan Holloran, Laurie Crowe, Carol Kerby, Debbie Belamy, Anna Ratliff, Tonya Hector, Susan Russell, Kristen Hunt, Christi Cearns, Roxane Attwood, Gina Granville, Carrie Chacon, Sue Shutak, Jane Norton, Phyllis Catrell, Abby Mayer and Gayla Artman.

Greg Russell, Richard Powell, Rick Valore and Anthony Ethridge contributed through encouragement, guidance or stories.

Marcel Venter helped with graphics; Luca Venter, my author photo; and Carolyn Drever, my website. Thank you for helping me look good in print and cyberspace!

Kim Bangs embraced the vision for this book, and the team at Regal Publishing brought it to fruition. Thank you.

Last of all, I'd like to thank my family for their patience and support. I love you all more than you will ever know.

Thank you, Pete, for being Mr. Mom while I was writing. I am so thankful for the myriad ways you encourage me in my dreams.

Peyton Marie, you made me a mom and have taught me much about life and love. Thank you for your sweet spirit and tender heart.

Morgan Anne, you continue to reinforce the lessons I flunked during Mom-Round One. I admire your spunk and passion for life.

INTRODUCTION

*A cup of coffee shared with a friend is happiness tasted
and time well spent.*
AUTHOR UNKNOWN

But seek first his kingdom and his righteousness.
MATTHEW 6:33

I am a coffee-drinkin' mama. A diaper-changing, laundry-washing, dinner-making, bath-giving, storytelling, big-time-loving, workin' mama. Let's face it: I need caffeine.

I started my relationship with coffee during finals week of my junior year in college. Faced with several tests to cram for, I needed to stay awake and alert. While I swigged caffeinated cola in the student union, my friend Ashley sipped cinnamon lattes and whipped cream-topped mochas.

"Just try it," she enticed, pushing her drink across the table through a sea of books and papers. "You will love it." Instantly, my soda lost its fizzle and her latte had lure. My life—and pocketbook—would never be the same.

It was love at first sip. Soon, my $1-a-day cola habit morphed into a $4-a-day latte routine. I started each crisp Colorado morning with a latte and a muffin on the way to my oh-so-early ten o'clock class, savoring every sip as my feet brushed through fallen multi-colored leaves.

Some 15 years later, my textbooks have found a cozy place in the basement. Most everything about my life has changed—except the coffee. Study groups have been replaced by playgroups; nights out replaced by bedtime roundups. I have a husband, two kids and credit card debt. Now I only dream of sleeping until ten o'clock; my mornings start at six.

The rooster crows early these days. Let's face it, most of us stumble to the coffee pot as soon as our feet hit the floor, seeking something to jumpstart our day. We live in a caffeinated world.

Coffee shops are commonplace, sometimes two or three in a city block. Every town likely has a post office, a mini mart and a coffee shop. My church even offers a full-service coffee bar. Coffee is in demand; everyone drinks coffee—college students, working professionals, men and women alike.

Moms are a huge contingent of the coffee guzzling gazillions. I'm right there with you, girlfriend. My stroller is equipped with cup holders so I can shop and sip. The grocery cart has a cup holder—convenient for that in-store Starbucks. Even my car has cup holders—but still, with all the places for me to put my coffee, I can rarely manage to keep it in the cup. If not drinking it, I'm spilling it.

Over the years, I have successfully spilled coffee on every surface known to man: countless shirts, a beautiful cream suit, my couch, my carpet and a very nice pair of suede shoes. Just the other day while trying to juggle groceries, my preschooler and a Frappuccino (hanging on by a straw), I tripped. I saved my child but dropped the bags and splattered iced coffee all over the side of my car—in a very busy parking lot. The worst part wasn't the broken eggs or humiliation, but that my tight schedule didn't allow time to grab a refill! (Sigh.)

I like coffee—I drink it every day—but there have been times when I put way too much faith in that little cup of caffeine. When my patience is as thin as the skin on an onion and my mood is swinging like playground equipment, I am reminded that I need Jesus to fill my cup, not the local barista. God has so much more for us than we realize. His power is available in big, joyous gulps, and yet most of us sip all the other things life offers, forgetting to drink in the fullness of God.

Learning to look to Jesus can be difficult. Busy moms seem to get a double dose of craziness between the corporate staircase and the carpool shuffle. Believe me, I know. Where do we find the time? How do we make our spiritual lives a priority? What does it look like to be filled by God? How might it actually transform our lives, our outlook and our parenting if we looked to Him every day?

This book offers encouragement to not so much "wake up and smell the coffee," but to wake up to an abundant life with God. So whether you have a penchant for coffee, diet soda, chai tea,

Red Bull or whatever, I suggest that there is something—or should I say Someone—better, ready to fill your cup.

Don't feel that you have to read the book straight through; if a certain chapter speaks to what is going on in your life, read it first. You need not read the chapters in order, just make sure to read 'em all.

Oh, and for maximum takeaway, savor the Questions to STIR and the Soul Sip Solutions at the end of each chapter. The Questions to STIR are designed to **S**timulate **T**houghtful **I**ntrospective **R**eflection, and it is my hope that the Soul Sip Solutions will challenge you to take action.

Finally, before we dive in, I'd like to make some introductions to the individuals you'll meet in this book: Pete, my husband of 11 years; Peyton, our older daughter, who is the wise age of nine; and four-year-old Morgan. The stories are not written in chronological order; so in one story, Peyton may be an infant, and in another, she is Big Sis with a curious sibling at her heels. My hope is that our family experiences will speak to you, no matter where you are in your mothering journey—and that you drink in the truths, challenges, laughter and joy universal to all moms.

Enjoy!
— CP

I

THIRSTY

Affirmation

✦✦✦

Life is a cup to be filled, not drained.
UNKNOWN

Let them give thanks to the Lord for his unfailing love and
his wonderful deeds for men, for he satisfies the thirsty
and fills the hungry with good things.
PSALM 107:8-9

"What's happening, Mom?" a white-faced Peyton yelped, bounding into our bedroom, her eyes big as swimming pools.

"Mommy! Mommy!" cried Morgan, who had also bolted from her bed, panicked. She sprinted toward me, arms outstretched.

What is happening? Is there an Army helicopter hovering over our house? I wondered. *Is it World War III?*

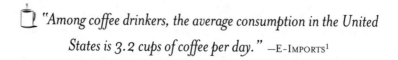

 "Among coffee drinkers, the average consumption in the United States is 3.2 cups of coffee per day." —E-IMPORTS[1]

The house seemed to be shaking like a football stadium with the opponent on fourth and goal; like a go-cart cranking at 100 miles per hour; like the washer on spin with a lopsided load. The echoing high-pitched whine was deafening. Our daughters were terrified. My husband and I looked at each other, bewildered. Then he smiled.

"It's the new coffeemaker," he said.

Hard to believe, but true. We'd just purchased one of those new-fangled, high-tech, grind-and-brew machines—the kind that offers the "freshest" cup you'll ever taste. It was supposed to "click on" before we awoke, producing a steaming pot of fresh java, ready to greet us at the prescribed early morning hour. What it hadn't promised was hearing loss and six months of post-traumatic stress therapy.

"I can't believe this coffee pot makes so much noise," I said, after reassuring the girls, tucking them back into bed and joining my husband in the kitchen.

"Me neither," said Pete. "What a disappointment."

What a disappointment. What had looked beautiful in the box turned out to be a whole lot different than I'd envisioned. Like a lot of things in life.

Becoming a Mom

Honestly, before becoming a mom, I had no idea what it would be like. As a confident young professional, I believed I could do it all—maintain romance in my marriage, keep a beautiful home, climb the corporate ladder *and* raise perfect children without a hitch or hiccup. Then I actually had children, and the evidence shows that I am not the mom I "expected" I'd be. I'm more like someone my younger self might have secretly judged to be subpar.

After the birth of my first child, it was all I could do to brush my teeth before two in the afternoon. I took Peyton to the grocery store in her jammies. I gave up on exercise and craved sleep like an addict. It didn't take long to see that I just couldn't—and still can't—do it all. If I cook dinner, the laundry piles up. If I wash clothes, the house stays a mess. If I spend time cleaning, I lose the opportunity to go to the park with my kids. Like a jigsaw puzzle purchased at a garage sale, my life as a mom always seems to be missing the few pieces that would make it complete.

"I never knew why you couldn't get it together," my sister-in-law told me once, reflecting on when she lived with our family just after Peyton was born. "Now that I'm a mom, I totally understand."

Until you are a mom, it is hard to really comprehend just how wonderful and precious and overwhelming and fatiguing parenting can be. The young, organized, professional me had no point of reference; my expectation for my mom-self was the high-gloss magazine version, lacking the reality of what is attainable—or even healthy.

According to Salary.com, the average mom works a 90-hour week.[2] *Ninety hours.* That is something my 55-hour "workaholic" younger self never dreamed of. (*Who's the slacker now?*) And though I am a good mom, sometimes the vision of what I thought I'd be haunts me like a phantom limb holding a bar I will never reach. Contrasting my expectations of what might have been with reality is a toxic cocktail that leaves a bitter taste and robs me of the joy of being a mom.

Life is different for moms today. We are busier than previous generations, and our kids are busier too. Life often throws us more than we can hit, like machine-launched to-do tennis balls coming at us in rapid succession. We keep swinging our "Perfect Mom" racquet, running ourselves to the brink of collapse, trying to hit (or juggle?) all the balls. Then we feel like a failure when we miss, wondering despite all our effort if what we do even makes a difference.

He Satisfies the Thirsty

Well, moms do make a difference. Career moms, stay-at-home working moms, single moms, married moms—we all do. And despite fatigue and frustration, we are always accountable for our actions and example. We rise early and retire late, busy with menial tasks forgotten by day's end, even with all the high-tech helps of today's consumer culture (jet-engine coffee maker, case in point). The depth and breadth of the difference we make may never be completely affirmed. We do it anyway. We do it because that's what love does.

Still, in the hustle and bustle of the day, subsisting on vanilla lattes, it is easy to forget about love and feel unappreciated and fragile, and even a little cranky. Considering my 90-hour workweek, it is not uncommon for me to have a latte in the morning and then forget (or not take time) to eat until I feel shaky and queasy in the afternoon. Once the caffeine and sugar are metabolized and there is still a mountain of laundry to tackle—what do you and I need to do? Where do we turn?

We turn to God.

Looking to God for our value and worth gives us a truer perspective of what matters. Most of us have chosen to be wives and mothers. We love our families and want the best for them—so we do the work. Feeling unappreciated and less than perfect, chased by ghost expectations, is not what God wants for us.

Good moms are not defined by folded laundry, clean toilets, gourmet meals or dust-free bookcases.

Though I definitely have my "woe is me" moments when I hoard the Red Vines and grumble like Eeyore, when I am centered on Jesus, my daily frustrations don't bother me as much. In fact, when I am rooted in God's truth, I feel affirmed in all I do. He whispers the truth that good moms are not defined by folded laundry, clean toilets, gourmet meals or dust-free bookcases. He reminds me that loving moms may not always have perfectly coiffed (or even clean) hair, shiny manicures or smooth legs; but they are marked by happy, healthy children, a solid sense of purpose and their calling to the job of motherhood and its fundamental, inherent value. When I am walking by faith, I am a better mom; I am more apt to be uplifting to others; I am honoring to my husband; and I am a fun-filled, all-around happy person.

A Cup of Affirmation

God loves us and says in His Word, the Bible, that He has a plan for each of us. Before we were born, He knew we would be mothers. He tells us, "Before I formed you in the womb I knew you, before you were born I set you apart" (Jeremiah 1:5). We were each created for a unique purpose, and a big part of that is our calling as mothers.

This is a huge thought. On days when I feel run down, I can hardly imagine God creating me for this job description. I feel like a clueless hopeful on *American Idol*, someone who can't sing but still wants to win the contest. Yet, despite my failings, God has grace for me—and for us all. "But to each one of us grace has been given" (Ephesians 4:7). God's grace is simply the ability to do what we can't accomplish in our own strength.

Jesus tells us to "let [our] light shine before men, that they may see [our] good deeds and praise [our] Father in heaven" (Matthew 5:16). We have the opportunity to show God's love to our children every day. We can be His eyes in seeing the best in them, His ears in listening with attentiveness, His voice in praise. We can be God's hands in molding, His arms in holding, His heart in loving our children. God's light shines through us even, and especially, when we are with our children. When I have my arms around the warmth of this truth, I am confident that what I do makes a difference, that my contribution is eternally significant. As a mom, I have come to intrinsically understand something the "confident young professional" didn't see: that I matter, because I matter to God.

Questions to STIR

1. What are your biggest frustrations? What triggers throw you off balance, and how can you avoid them?

2. How do you know that you matter? To what or to whom do you look for your value, affirmation and worth?

3. As moms, God's light shines in and through us. How does this truth change your perspective on the day-to-day details?

Soul Sip Solutions

1. Take a moment to remember (and appreciate!) the value you bring as a mom. List the blessings you bring to your family. These can be as simple as "Makes a fabulous meatloaf" or "Gives great hugs!"

2. One day this week, go for a walk in lieu of a "pick-me-up" latte. Breathe deeply. Find refreshment in the crisp air, and check in with God.

3. If you feel overwhelmed and discouraged, consider a simple prayer like this: "Dear God, I need You. Please show me that I matter as a mom—and that I matter to You. Amen." God hears your prayers.

Reflection and Challenge

How did it go? What did you learn? Record your thoughts. If you didn't get to it, take heart. We all have those times. Pray and seek God's next step for you in this area.

_____

_____

_____

_____

_____

_____

_____

_____

_____

_____

_____

_____

_____

_____

_____

_____

_____

_____

_____

_____

2

THE DAILY GRIND

Rest

My candle burns at both its ends;
It will not last the night;
But oh, my foes, and oh, my friends—
It gives a lovely light.
EDNA ST. VINCENT MILLAY

Come to me, all you who are weary and burdened, and I will give you rest.
MATTHEW 11:28

I am absolutely, positively, 100 percent, without a doubt, mom's honor, "double-Frappuccino-with-whipped cream-and-a-cherry-on-top" sure that drive-thru coffee stops were created for moms. And I'll bet you they were created by a mom too.

Only a mom knows the challenge of getting a coffee with little ones in tow: Fix hair, apply lip gloss, pop a breath mint, unbuckle car seat, grab toddler and retrieve carrier with sleeping infant, diaper bag, purse, and tissues (in case of a sneeze emergency); then balance all of this like a circus performer, negotiate the doors, wait in line, get coffee and return to the car without spilling. Truly, the "Coffee-Mom March" should be an Olympic event!

The advent of the coffee drive-thru arguably equals the invention of the stroller. The benefits are clear: I don't have to get out of the car, do my hair or put on lipstick. For morning coffee runs, I can leave the kids in their pajamas, hop in the car, hit the drive-thru and cruise home—without event or aggravation. There are no kids to haul, no bags to sling—just drive up and order the deliciously convenient sanity-in-a-cup.

But there's more! Using a hands-free earpiece, I can talk on the phone, catching up with my mom or sister, file my nails, do a grocery list and apply a little touch of mascara while waiting in the queue! (It's okay; we've all done it.) Moms are multitasking machines, and our minds are cranking at high-speed long before we get to the coffee shop, drive-thru or not. Even in our uncaffeinated moments, we are always on the go.

"On average, a drive-through business with a great location can sell 250 cups of espresso and coffee drinks each day."

—E-Imports[1]

The Rat Race

Snuggled in the heart of Northern California's Napa Valley, on a girls' weekend escape, I learned her secret. It wasn't a secret really, just an amazing factoid that immediately bonded us like sisters.

"I have a rat in my head," Kellie blurted as we sat munching pizza. The group all stared, stunned, slices of pizza in midair.

"A rat?" someone clarified.

"Yep, a rat." She smiled. "He runs on a wheel inside my brain, and he never stops. My mind is always racing," Kellie explained. "I am always thinking about what I need to do, where I need to be, what I need at the grocery store—I can't get him to stop."

So that was it. A rat. I knew that rodent. I had one nestled in my own noggin—running and running on a never-ending treadmill. While some of the girls just laughed, I was incredulous. Immediately, I found in Kellie—and her busy rat—a kindred spirit, someone wired the same way as me. Poor girl.

After our weekend, I thought a lot about my cerebral rat: why he runs, what feeds him and why he seems so at home in my head. I'd like to say that I'm ambitious and enterprising and that cerebral rats thrive in creative environments, but that is a self-deluded pile of meadow muffins. My rat keeps me up nights, captive and miserable. He steals precious moments that I should share with my children and robs me of relaxation. He is no family pet; he is no friend of mine.

I decided to name my rat Templeton, after the infamous, gluttonous, trash-eating rodent in *Charlotte's Web*. Remember Templeton? He spent his nights scurrying and scavenging, feeding on fairground rubbish. He was helpful at times, but mostly he was just a fat nuisance. My Templeton is also a hungry—and irritating—fella. What feeds him? It is not leftover hot dogs and discarded cotton candy. Oh no. My rat runs on the need to please and the need to perform.

As Templeton runs, he generates the "need tos" that fill my mind: I need to do laundry, go to the grocery and call my sister-in-law; I need to get in shape, organize my closet and finish that spreadsheet. I need to . . . I need to . . . I need to. The thoughts never stop, so I make lists to clear my head. Pages upon pages. Single-spaced. Running my life by a list gives me an amazing sense of accomplishment: the more items I check off, the more productive I feel. So I spend my days doing, crossing things off the list.

Unfortunately, Templeton never stops. Even if I get some to-dos accomplished, he, like the class gossip, just runs with something else. The trash he feeds on does not satiate. It is never enough. I always feel that I could, and should, do more. As Templeton runs, so I run—a slave to the perpetual list.

The Treadmill Wheel

Rat or no rat, I bet you've made a list or two and—though you may be slow to admit it—even skipped a shower on occasion because you were so darn overscheduled. If I had coordinating shoes and bags to match all the hats I wear, I could double as a women's millinery.

Life coach Cheryl Richardson says, "We live in a rest-averse culture that abhors inactivity and reinforces the belief that our value as human beings is directly related to what we accomplish."[2] Our value related to what we accomplish . . . talk about misplaced self-worth! What is even more heartbreaking is that we buy it.

Although our roles may vary from day to day, most of us juggle them all at some point: wife, mother, employee, teacher, chef, nurse, maid, cheerleader, administrative assistant, CFO, architect, personal shopper, interior designer, leader, landscaper, psychologist, counselor, advisor, volunteer, daughter, friend and, of course, chauffeur. Phew! From food to finances we manage the mayhem. For married moms, husbands share the monumental parenting load. For single moms, it is likely a one-woman show.

It is easy to see how we get so worn out. I grab caffeine throughout my day because it is a tasty treat—but also because I erroneously believe it will help sustain my energy level. The truth is, I am tired to my core. Every bit of me is tired. Even my hair is tired. My conditioner bottle reads, "Years of blow-drying, perms, and even pregnancy have fatigued your hair." (The marketers are close, but it is *post*-pregnancy life that has fatigued me—and my hair—the most.) The conditioner promises "renewal" from root to tip, so I slather the stuff all over my hair and body to test its restorative powers, but neither conditioner nor caffeine really does the trick.

A Cup of Rest

There is no quick fix. Much like staying out of the chocolate chip cookies, slowing down our life and our thoughts takes awareness and resolve. Old habits are hard to overcome. Change takes time, but success is attainable if we focus on what matters most.

I have to admit, at times I run so fast that I have trouble hearing the sweet whispers that could help slow me down—and last I checked God wasn't communicating via BlackBerry. What a bummer; if that were the case, I'd be online with Him all the time, if you know what I mean.

Here's the scoop: Though I'd like to control and direct every aspect of my life, I fall short even on my best days. My maestro attempts are anxiety-ridden and poorly executed. God has a much better plan for me—for all of us.

My favorite Bible verse is Matthew 6:33: "But seek first his kingdom and his righteousness, and all these things will be given to you as well." To me this says, *Put Me first. Take time for Me and I'll take care of you. I've got you, got your kids, your schedule, what's for dinner, the whole deal. Just take time for Me. Seek Me first.*

God knows how crazy life is. He is patient. He loves us despite what we do or how we perform. (Wahoo! Grab the Bon Bons and hit the couch!) He forgives our failures and misguided actions. He just wants our hearts.

"When we rest in Jesus, the craziness of this world will not mark us internally."

—GREG THOMPSON, PASTOR, SMOKY HILL VINEYARD

The need to please drives the rat, but it is our relationship with Jesus that ultimately brings peace and fulfillment. In *The Purpose Driven Life*, bestselling author Rick Warren reminds us, "God is far more interested in what you are than what you do. We are human *beings*, not human doings."[3] When we slow down and accept God's unconditional love, a new life begins.

Slowing the wheel takes minute-to-minute walking with God and trusting Him. Proverbs 3:5-6 says, "Trust in the LORD with all your heart and lean not on your own understanding; in all your ways acknowledge him, and he will make your paths straight."

A straight path. That seems like a galaxy away from my congested, hairpin-curvy highway, but it gives me hope—hope that I can find true rest from the daily grind. My pastor, Greg Thompson, says, "When we rest in Jesus, the craziness of this life will not mark us internally." I like that.

Going to the coffee pot in the morning is as routine as putting on my glasses or brushing my teeth. It's an established habit; it's how I start my day. While I sometimes feel as if I don't have time for God, I always seem to have time for coffee. As my nine-year-old would say, "That's messed up."

What if I went straight to my Bible every day along with the coffee pot? What if I looked to Jesus, filled my cup, and took "quick sips" of His Word over my lunch break or while waiting at tennis practice? It would be life-changing, and no doubt provide me the rest from the rat race I so desperately crave.

Questions to STIR

1. Do you have a rat (or even a lazy hamster) generating "need tos" in your life? What needs and assumptions propel their activity?

2. How comfortable are you with slowing down and taking time for yourself? Any time spent with God or caring for yourself might make you a better mom. How does this change your paradigm?

3. What does it mean to "rest in Jesus"? In what ways can you trust God more with the details of your everyday life?

Soul Sip Solutions

1. Rip up your to-do list for a day. If you can't do that, then limit the need-to items to five per day.

2. Think about where you can find rest from the rat race. Carve out a few minutes to sit in the sun, nap or read. Take a break. Reflect on how God factors into your life equation.

3. Read from the book of Psalms and the book of Proverbs (you don't have to read at length) each morning along with your cup of coffee. Pray, and surrender your agenda to God.

Reflection and Challenge

Were you able to slow down? Look back at your Soul Sip Solutions and record what impacted you the most.

_____

_____

_____

_____

_____

_____

3

LATTE LETDOWN

Grace

Life is under no obligation to give us what we expect.
MARGARET MITCHELL

*My grace is sufficient for you, for my power is made
perfect in weakness.*
2 CORINTHIANS 12:9

Don't you just hate it when you drive across town to your favorite
coffee house, wait in line, shell out $4 for a latte and then your first
dearly anticipated sip tastes crummy? It's the pits. When I spend
hard-earned cash for a coffee drink, I want it piping hot and delicious, from the first sip to the last. Lukewarm lattes, burnt-tasting
espresso, too much (or too little) syrup and even a leaky cup can
ruin my coffee experience. What's worse, this "latte letdown" can
taint my whole day if I let it.

 Caffé latte: *one part espresso, two parts milk* Cappuccino:
equal parts espresso and milk with frothed milk on top

—MARTHA STEWART LIVING, JANUARY 2008[1]

If coffee promises energy, then disappointed expectations bode
exasperation. Whenever I go into something expecting too much
or wanting a perfect result, I, like a girl on a blind date, am bound

for a letdown. This happens more than I care to admit. Everything—from wanting my hair to look great or cooking a delicious dinner, to enjoying the perfect coffee—is subject to my expectations. And this, my friends, is a recipe for disaster.

Cheese Sandwiches

"Mom," my daughter Peyton says to me at the bus stop, "we are having a Valentine's party at school. You can help if you want."

Translation: *If you love me and are a good mom, you will volunteer to help with the Valentine's Day party.*

"You could make the heart-shaped cheese sandwiches like Kendall's mom made last year. I really liked those."

Translation: *A store-bought container of sugar cookies is not going to cut it; you need to step up like other moms and figure out something darn special.*

When did the stakes get so high? My daughter is only in grade school, yet time spent volunteering in the classroom can equal a part-time job. Now, I adore my daughter, but as she was gearing up for first grade, I must admit I was a teensy-weensy bit excited about the space her "school days" might create in my schedule. (I was, in retrospect, delusional.)

The first week she came home with more papers and volunteer opportunities than I could count. I could be: a Parent Helper in the classroom, serve on the Student Advisory Council, attend work parties to prepare school material, cut Box Tops or help with the Book Fair! The coup de grâce was the opportunity to be an administrative assistant in the office. Though needing an assistant of my own, the expectation is: *Good parents help.* So I signed up.

Now, however, like a knock-kneed cowboy, I am often not sure where to draw the line. While I appreciate the effort other parents contribute, they're starting to make me look bad. An attempt to save time grabbing store-bought cookies doesn't cut it. In fact, I am expected to bring custom cookie-cutter heart-shaped sandwiches with mustard, thank you very much.

The expectations for moms today are high. Some expectations are realistic; some are not. Some are imposed and some we conjure up ourselves. And as we strive to meet humanly impossible expectations, we often fall short. Comparison and the need for perfection carry the risk of feeling like we never measure up; believing that we are failures squelches the spontaneous joy that gurgles up in life's unsuspecting moments. How easily we disappoint others—and ourselves—when we let these "works" define us.

The Perfect Outcome

What are your expectations? Do they move you forward or set you up for disappointment? Not long ago, four of my best girlfriends and I decided to treat ourselves to massages at a prestigious spa. When we arrived at the resort, we changed into our robes and made our way to the "relaxation room." One by one, each friend was called for her massage, and soon I was left waiting by myself. Instead of relaxing, I became irritated. I sat calculating, by the minute, what it was costing to sit in the *relaxation* chair. When the therapist finally arrived, she apologized for her delay, but I was miffed.

I later realized that my inability to let go of a "perfect outcome" ruined the whole experience. The spa with friends (sans kids) was time to be treasured, but I let my out-of-whack expectations ruin the day.

A Cup of Grace

Our schedules demand that we be ruthless about priorities. Deciding what matters most means defining our priorities based on our values and examining our subsequent actions. It isn't that I don't value the cheese sandwiches that Kendall's mom makes, but I choose to spend the extra hour on a bike ride with Peyton. Kendall's mom may choose to make sandwiches with her daughter. Good for her. There is no one right way to parent, no set of priorities better than another. The best set of priorities is rooted in one's values, which will vary from person to person, from family to family.

Problems loom large when I adopt someone else's expectations. A few times I've tried to bring the cheese-sandwich equivalent, attempting to be the ultimate mom. Yet when I deviate from what I feel is best, I end up frustrated. I need to give myself some grace. I don't need to be the cheese-sandwich mom.

"Grace is having a commitment to—or at least an acceptance of—being ineffective and foolish."[2] This quote, from Anne Lamott's book *Traveling Mercies*, reminds me that I don't have to be perfect, and no one else does either. Life is messy, and I often tumble, expectations and all, like a fast-pedaling toddler on a tricycle.

Unrealistic expectations set us up for disappointment, make us crazy and steal our joy. This is, at heart level, a spiritual problem. The answer is to acknowledge that God's grace extends to us all; we are all in process, and there is grace in adjusting and readjusting our self-expectations and priorities.

John 8:36 says that if the Son [Jesus] sets us free, "you will be free indeed." We can be free of the chains that weigh us down—including false expectations and perfectionism—through the power of Jesus in our lives. Let's face it: Parenting, unrealistic expectations and parental peer pressure can be Tough, with a capital T. Affirming personal priorities and achieving freedom from the world's expectations require releasing any worry about what others think; once we do this, we discover that God has something much better.

Without God, our individual cups are filled with cold, stale coffee. Our human tendency is to judge; and as such, we are limited in our capacity to fill each other's cup. God alone knows our heart, and He will never fail. He sees our uniqueness and is always there, always loving us. First Samuel 16:7 says, "The LORD does not look at the things man looks at. Man looks at the outward appearance, but the LORD looks at the heart."

Acknowledging and accepting that our value is determined by God frees us from the dictates of others and gives us the freedom to love without strings, starting with ourselves. When we let Jesus fill our cup, we find freedom from the need to please, and freedom from perfectionism and expectations. We don't have to be perfect. We are given grace—"For it is by grace you have been saved" (Ephesians 2:8)—and by grace we are forgiven. We can relax, assured that we are loved just as we are. *Just as we are*—now that's what I call grace.

Questions to STIR

1. Think about the expectations you have for yourself in different areas of your life. How do your expectations affect your performance, outlook and perception of yourself? In what areas can you let go of a perfect (or idealized) outcome?

2. Who or what are you allowing to establish your worth? Ask God for His grace to see your value through His eyes. What are signs of God's grace in your life?

3. Where do you seek to fill your cup—achievements, cute clothes, cheese sandwiches? Explore the ways in which God can fill your cup to overflowing.

Soul Sip Solutions

1. List the expectations you carry in every area of your life: mom, wife, employee, classroom volunteer, and so on. Include seemingly trivial expectations and assumptions. Now circle the ones you impose on yourself. Cross out the ones imposed by others. Highlight the valid and healthy ones. Pray that God will guide you with regard to balancing healthy expectations.

2. Look up the definition of "grace" in the dictionary. Now read Ephesians 2:8 in the Bible. God offers us grace, despite our failings and imperfections. What does this truth mean to you?

3. This week praise imperfection, effort and good intention. Let go of unhealthy expectations and try to live more fully in the favor and grace offered by God.

Reflection and Challenge

What Soul Sip Solutions did you try? What defines "perfect" for you? How do your expectations influence your children?

_____

_____

_____

_____

_____

_____

COFFEE BREAK
WITH SUSAN

Dear Moms,

When our boys were in primary school, we moved to a house with a colossal, kid-friendly backyard. It was a perfect space for two young boys; and in the years we lived there, the grass was well worn! The house, however, was much larger than I'd bargained for, and it soon became a burden rather than a blessing. The tasks of scrubbing, dusting, vacuuming and dusting again, were never ending.

Convinced that every mom worth her weight in dish soap kept an immaculately clean, well-organized home, I was determined to outdo them all! Housework soon took priority over time with my boys, my husband and time for me.

Then one summer afternoon, while I was knee-deep in rubber gloves and toilet cleaner, God got my attention through a strategically placed note, written by my eight-year-old son:

Hi Mom,

Do you think that if you're not too busy today you could bring out some apple juice and sit with us under the big tree? Maybe you could stay and pitch to us for just a while 'cause I'm getting real good at hitting! But if you don't have time, that's okay.
I love you, Josh

The gloves came off! Through the endearing words of a child, God graced me with a wake-up call, reminding me of the riches right before me, and the missed moments I would never get back.

Endless daily tasks will always be there, but the time with your children will end. You have them but for a *moment*. Seize each one! Recognize that your riches don't lie in a perfectly kept house, an award-winning casserole, or a made-from-scratch, home-baked pie, but in the investment you make in the life of your children, and the fullness of life you've been graced with in them. Life is busy. The question is: What are we busy with?

Love to you,
Susan Holloran

4

A TRUE BREW

Courage

*Courage doesn't always roar. Sometimes courage is the little voice
at the end of the day that says I'll try again tomorrow.*
MARY ANNE RADMACHER

*I command you—be strong and courageous! Do not be afraid or
discouraged. For the LORD your God is with you wherever you go.*
JOSHUA 1:9, NLT

When I finally reached the counter, I ordered the largest latte on
the menu—triple shot.

"Need something to wake you up?" the barista asked with
a smile.

"Something like that," I replied. I turned to my daughter, to
change the subject. "Peyton, do you want anything?"

"Um, I'll have a vanilla steamer," she told the barista.

"Kid-temp," I reminded.

Once we had our drinks, we made our way to the car. *A wake-
me-up?* I'd already had that; I'd started the morning with a gargan-
tuan cup of worry, four pumps of liquid angst and a sprinkling of
foreboding. The effects of the cocktail were clearly evident in my
system, not only giving me a tight, 50-pound chest, but a full-
fledged anxiety buzz. I was awake, no doubt about that.

I wasn't sure why I'd even stopped for coffee. I sure didn't
need the caffeine. Perhaps I was wanting a bit of comfort, some
simple assurance that I'd get exactly what I wanted—at least here.

Taking Peyton for this upcoming appointment was a whole other equation. I didn't know what to expect or what the outcome would be.

As we drove, I engaged my daughter in small talk, as if we were on an awkward first date—tentative and nervous.

"Nice day today, don't you think? You can see the mountains perfectly."

"What are you learning in school this week?"

"Where do you want to go to lunch?"

I asked the questions, mostly to keep my mind occupied; left to silence or a radio backdrop, my thoughts would have been kidnapped by fear, the kind that hijacks your gray matter at every stoplight and intersection, eventually taking over your being like a four-lane highway.

When we arrived at our destination, Peyton and I got out of the car and started to walk in. I looked at her. She had finished her steamer and left the skeleton cup in the drink holder of her booster seat; I was still clutching my latte.

"Wait a second," I told her and ducked back into the car. I set my coffee in the console and relocked the car. Then I grabbed her hand.

"So let's see what the doctor says," I told her. And we walked into the office.

"Without belittling the courage with which men have died, we should not forget the courage with which men . . . have lived. The courage of life is often a less dramatic spectacle than the courage of a final moment; but it is no less a magnificent mixture of triumph and tragedy. . . ." —John F. Kennedy[1]

Moxie and Then Some

It takes a lot of courage to be a mom. No matter where you live or how old your children are, I am sure you've had your fair share of trying times. Let's face it: whether assessing a skinned knee or holding your child while he or she is immunized, mothering takes bravery. Lots of it. As soon as the doctor hands us our firstborn, we are forever changed, instantly transported to the Land of Big Love, where all the rules we once knew are void; our hearts grow to encompass infinite hope for the prosperity and happiness of our children, and with it, fear of loss, fear of failure and the fear that we won't be adequate to the challenge.

The role of mom involves risk-taking and making choices that will determine the health and livelihood of our children. The food we buy and prepare, the safety of our home environment, our discipline practices—it all matters. Every decision, every reaction matters. (No pressure.) This is not a class we can drop or a career choice we can change; once a mom, there is no turning back, so we muster the moxie and do our best.

It is scary. Some days, I don't feel like I have enough control of my own life to guide another person's development. Other days, it seems like I have it all together, and then my little one will dart out into a parking lot. When I envision what could have happened, my all-together façade crumbles, and worry closes in, visiting like an old relative I don't like but can't refuse.

There are many variables in the mom equation, factors we must figure out as we go: How do you (after volunteering for a "simple" task) figure out how to construct 25 houses out of graham crackers for your child's kindergarten class? How do you change a blow-out diaper without getting poop in your baby's hair—or your own? What do you do when you run into an old flame at the grocery store . . . and then realize that you are still wearing your "Weight Watchers" nametag? What do you do when your toddler traces the varicose veins in your legs with a finger or tells you Barbie has bigger boobies than you? Or chokes on a Tater Tot? You do what other moms do: You keep your head and keep mothering. It takes mettle, but thankfully, we are not alone in the journey.

Following the Lion

In the well-known Narnia book *The Horse and His Boy*, C. S. Lewis tells the story of a young fellow who runs away from his childhood home in search of a better life. During his travels he faces many obstacles, challenges and trials—several times fearing for his life when chased by a mighty lion. Near the end of the book, Aslan, the great Lion, meets up with the boy. When the boy shares of the many lions stalking him, Aslan replies, "There was only one lion . . . I was the lion." Aslan proceeds to explain that he was the lion who stood by him and protected him, even chased him when needed, in order to keep him from danger.[2]

During the last year, I've been reading the Narnia series with my older daughter, and I've found that the themes have great takeaway. This particular story has had a profound impact. You see, like the boy, many times I've felt alone and afraid—especially on the sometimes-solitary journey of motherhood. Whether I feel anxious for the health of my children, am stuck in traffic, am late for a meeting or am frustrated that I don't see the productivity I once did as a working professional, parenting can be a tough road. I often feel, despite all the other moms I know, that no one can quite identify with my particular situation; in the midst of family and friends, I feel alone.

The thing is, I don't see the whole picture. I only see my small part of the story. But God is constantly watching out for me, like Aslan did for the boy. Maybe when I get stuck in traffic, there is an accident I have avoided. Perhaps when my children get the flu, they've been spared something much worse. God is always there in my struggles, whether I choose to see Him or not. He is the Lion, protecting, comforting and chasing me. And as such, I have no reason to fret. I am free to trust God and live my life with courage.

A Cup of Courage

Of course, this is much easier said than done. Just watch the evening news and angst sets in like a heavy fog. There is a lot of scary stuff out there. Worst-case scenarios flood my head. I know moms who hover and overprotect, limiting "risky" activities and foods; but their attempts to keep their children from harm limit life's joy—for them and for their children. This is not God's heart for us.

Joshua 1:9 says, "I command you—be strong and courageous! Do not be afraid or discouraged. For the LORD your God is with you wherever you go" (*NLT*). God is always with us. It is a promise, and with this promise is the freedom to face our fears and take action to go toward the life of our dreams.

"The Lord is the stronghold of my life—of whom should I be afraid?" —PSALM 27:1

God wants you to step out in faith and TRY—Trust and Respect Yourself! Have the personal integrity to decide what matters to you, take reasonable risks and go for it. Don't expect it to always be pretty; mistakes happen, kids get sick and the coffee (milk, juice, shampoo, laundry soap) will spill. We live in a broken world, and the reality is that no one gets through it without a hiccup or a mountain, but we can get through it with God's protection.

Franklin D. Roosevelt said in his First Inaugural Address on March 4, 1933, "Let me assert my firm belief that the only thing we have to fear is fear itself." Bingo. Fear robs us of the full life God intends for us. A better way is to look to the Lord each day, release our worries, pray and proceed with courage and quiet confidence, knowing that God's got our back.

Questions to STIR

1. As a mom, what areas of your life require the most courage?

2. What role does fear play in your life, especially as it relates to your child (children)? Do you ever limit activities due to a perceived risk of failure or injury?

3. In what ways do you try to control the outcomes of your life—or do you trust that God is in complete control?

Soul Sip Solutions

1. On a sheet of paper, list your fears. Pray about each item and release it to God. Pray that He would give you courage.

2. List one activity or aspiration you have not tried due to fear of failure. Put a plan in motion to pursue that goal.

3. Use a concordance (a reference tool often found in the back of a Bible) to look up the words "courage," "brave" and "trust," and write out the verses that impact you the most. Press in to God's heart. How can you trust Him more, and where in your life can you be more courageous?

Reflection and Challenge

What did you learn about overcoming your fears and trusting God? Record your thoughts.

_____

_____

_____

_____

_____

_____

_____

_____

_____

_____

_____

_____

5

A FINE BLEND

Friendship

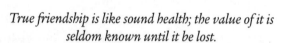

*True friendship is like sound health; the value of it is
seldom known until it be lost.*
CHARLES CALEB COLTON

*Oh, for the days when I was in my prime, when God's
intimate friendship blessed my house.*
JOB 29:4

SUBJECT: Dinner for BFFs
DAY/TIME: Monday, 9:07 A.M.
TO: Heather, Erika, Ashley and Carolyn
FROM: Celeste

Hey girls,
     How was your weekend? Miss U. Can we meet for dinner this
week? Maybe Wednesday?

REPLY FROM: Heather
     Sorry. Working late on Wed. night. Have conference call with
China office.

FROM: Celeste
     OK. How about Thursday?

REPLY FROM: Carolyn
     Sorry. Brent is traveling and I have to watch Jake. Thursday
doesn't work.

FROM: Celeste
   Friday?

REPLY FROM: Erika
   Have tickets to a concert. ☺ I'm out for Friday night.

FROM: Celeste
   It is impossible to coordinate schedules. Should we look to
next year? JK.

REPLY FROM: Ashley
   What about meeting for coffee at 8 A.M. on Saturday?

REPLY FROM: Heather
   Works for me.

REPLY FROM: Carolyn
   Me too.

REPLY FROM: Erika.
   In. I will bring pictures from my Italy trip!

SUBJECT: Coffee Date for BFFs
DAY/TIME: Monday, 2:14 P.M.
TO: Heather, Erika, Ashley and Carolyn
FROM: Celeste

Finally! See you guys on Sat. morning for coffee!

BFFs and Busy Lives

It can be hard to find time for friends. Often, just trying to keep
milk in the fridge and clean underwear in rotation, I seldom have
time for a casual dinner with pals who have equal demands on
their lives. It is akin to getting 20 three-year-olds to nap at the
same time.
   But *friendship* is so important.

When I was in college, my gal pals and I were together almost 24-7. We went to class together, studied, shopped and roomed together. However, things have changed. Some of us are now married with kids, some are engaged, others still single. We all have different jobs and live in different parts of the city. Our priorities, even values, have changed—and like an invisible force, our hectic lives conspire to pull us away from the very friendships that help sustain us.

Need to cheer up a friend? Make some cookies and wrap them up with a pound of your favorite coffee!

We can't let this happen. Though I could write an entire book on friendship, what I want to emphasize is this: Women need friends. Good girlfriends. We need other women in our life who encourage us, understand us and support us. And we must fight for these friendships.

Consider Erika, one of my best friends from college. She is always involved in the social scene and knows someone everywhere. If we go skiing, she'll run into a friend on the slopes. If we go shopping, she'll see someone she knows. We've been friends for almost 20 years, and yet our lives are now very different. We live more than 45 minutes apart; she, in the city, and I, in the suburbs. We both have very busy schedules and find it difficult to get together.

Then there is Monica, a friend I met a few years ago at church. Our third-graders are best friends. She lives five minutes away and I see her all the time because our lives naturally cross paths. It would be very easy to let my friendship with Erika slip away, "replaced" by my relationship with Monica. But that would be a devastating mistake. I value Erika; she brings me a fresh perspective and a history I don't have with Monica.

I see this happen all the time. Women marry, have kids and fall into the crevasse of busyness, letting friendships lapse, never to be seen by their pals again.

Maintaining Connections

Why are friends so important? They bring us understanding, an honest voice and a shoulder to lean on. Friends laugh with us and encourage us. We do the same for them. Having a friend means being a friend (see Proverbs 18:24); maintaining the relationship is a shared responsibility of anticipating needs and making the effort.

There is also grace in true friendship. Friendships change over time and may not always be conveniently maintained by email and voicemail alone. Those who know me best realize that I am usually not quick to return calls. My pals know that I love them, and if I've not responded to a message, I will call them when my life slows down. In the past, they might have wondered if I was upset, but now, they just give me space—and grace—and know I'll make the effort when I can. And I do the same for them.

But we do have to make an effort. My best pals and I take a *girls* trip once a year, go to dinner every month or so and participate in a book club together. Of course, we see each other randomly, but the dinners and getaways are scheduled into our lives well in advance to help keep us truly connected with quality time—time when we can share our hearts, remind each other of dreams, ask tough questions and exchange valuable feedback.

I am a better person thanks to my friends. My husband realizes this and is supportive of my time away. I, in turn, encourage (most of) his fishing trips and golf outings with his guy pals.

📖 *"Research cited in* Vital Friends *by Tom Rath claims that workplace friendships could make you seven times more satisfied with your job."*

—*LADIES' HOME JOURNAL*[1]

Lasting friendships are not easily sustained, but the investment pays big dividends. My friends have helped shape who I am: Erika keeps me youthful and up-to-date; Carolyn reminds me to find the positive in every situation; Ashley models discipline and fitness; Heather helps me breathe when I'm stressed; Monica prays with and for me. Each knows my dreams and pushes me toward them. They also know my fears and burdens, and so I never walk alone, whether on a mountaintop or in the deep underbrush of the valley.

A Cup of Friendship

Of course, as amazing as they are, my friends are not perfect. (But don't tell them I said so.) Sometimes they don't answer the phone when I really, really need them to, buried in *their* stuff when *I* need attention. Sometimes, though not often, they may tell me what I *want* to hear, not what I *need* to hear.

There is only one true and lasting friend who is always available. He understands me and wants the best for me. He not only inspires me, but He sustains and equips me. He tells me the truth, straight-up, all the time. He is Jesus.

I'm embarrassed to admit it, but I used to see my relationship with Jesus as a duty, a chore to be crossed off a list. I'd think, *I need to have my Bible study today* or *I need to pray* so that I could feel like I was "growing" spiritually. I actually approached my relationship with God like a Monday through Friday job. I'd do Bible study five days a week and take weekends off. And, if I took a "sick day" now and then, or forgot, well, I just figured the Big Boss would understand.

He does understand, but what He wanted me to get, that I (finally!) now get, is: *He is my friend.* A relationship with Jesus is not a checklist duty. I don't call my friends because I feel like I need to, I call them because I want to—and it's no different with God.

Friendships don't grow when we feel forced into them; they grow when our hearts connect. When I came to understand, to truly understand, that God wants me to talk with Him all the time—about ordinary stuff—not just requests or ritual, I became His friend. My heart connected with His. I now look forward to talking with Him 24-7, whether it is first thing in the morning, in the car, at work or the last thing at night. Jesus is the go-to friend who never fails and who loves at all times (see Proverbs 17:17).

Questions to STIR

1. Who are your best friends? How have they blessed and encouraged you? What kind of a friend are you to them?

2. Have you let friendships slip away due to busyness or apathy? If so, what might you do to reconnect?

3. Do you see Jesus as a true friend or a duty to cross off your list?

Soul Sip Solutions

1. List your three best friends. Write each one a handwritten note and tell them what they mean to you. Send it snail mail. (Sorry, no email.)

2. List the qualities you want in a friend. Think about all that Jesus offers. Then set aside some time to talk with Him—just about life—like you would with a best friend.

3. Think about how you approach your relationship with Jesus. If you view prayer or Bible study as a duty, how might you change your perspective?

Reflection and Challenge

How did the Soul Sip challenges go? What did you learn? Rejoice in your progress (even baby steps) and be patient with yourself. Give God permission to continue to speak to you and lead you in this area.

_____

_____

_____

_____

_____

_____

6

A SHOT OF LAUGHTER

Humor

When we begin to take our failures non-seriously, it means we are ceasing to be afraid of them. It is of immense importance to learn to laugh at ourselves.
KATHERINE MANSFIELD

He will yet fill your mouth with laughter and your lips with shouts of joy.
JOB 8:21

The coffee line was exceptionally long. The kind of long you think just *m-a-y-b-e* isn't worth your time, but you stay anyway because the thought of that first steamy-hot sip melts all your icy arguments. This morning, I most definitely did not have the time, but here I was, six people back, waiting, desperate for a tasty cup of yum. The earthy aroma of roasted coffee beans romanced my nose, triggering a Pavlovian response; I was reduced to dogged obedience, standing in line to retrieve my beloved mocha.

I had never seen the place so busy—it was like a day at the zoo; in fact, it *was* a zoo. The hum of activity hijacked my ears: moms chatting, oblivious to their toddlers circling their chairs like frisky pups; business types tapping on laptops; teens texting messages, their fingers flashing at a pace once known only to cartoon superheroes. Countless people on their way to work stood, arms crossed, feet tapping, impatient. And right behind me stood a man my single pals might've called a "hottie." (I, of course, being happily married, hardly noticed.)

As I got close to the counter, though, my stomach dropped like a roller coaster. No, I didn't leave the iron on or forget to shut the garage—I simply realized I was low on cash. Really low. I'd spent my last $10 the night before getting a quick dinner for my kids. And I'd made a pact with my husband to not charge anything more this month on our credit/debit cards. What was I to do?

I dug around in my purse. My wallet was buried under a brush, several fast-food napkins, hair clips, a lipgloss, a variety of pens and the kitchen sink. I finally retrieved $3. With the loose coins at the bottom of my handbag circus, I knew I'd have enough. I had to have enough. I'd waited in line too long to abandon my coffee crusade now.

I ordered my coffee and dug for the change. The cashier waited. I found two quarters and a nickel. I just needed one more dime. I dug some more. The people behind me waited. I could feel their stares.

Then I saw it. I caught a glimpse of the precious coin, wedged in the seam of my bag. I couldn't quite grab it, so I tipped my purse sideways and jiggled the coin loose. It fell into my hand . . . and, in the same moment, my "emergency" tampon fell out onto the floor, bouncing off the shoe of the man standing behind me.

Mistakes and Mishaps

It could have been worse. Certain times of the month, I have a whole stockpile of tampons in my purse.

While I'd like to say that this incident is unique, it is not. Self-humiliation, like brushing my teeth, is routine. They don't always equal this spectacle, but similar moments abound. Sometimes I feel slow and outrageously klutzy: Late for a lunch date, I'll miss a stair and trip just as I enter the restaurant. I'll forget to shave my legs for a week and then, without thinking, pull on a skirt for work. I'll spill a drink on my meeting notes. I'll accidentally leave leftover Chinese food in my car overnight and then have to pick up my boss for a ride-along business call with my car smelling like I've had killer gas.

You can't make this stuff up. This is my life.

The thing is, I'm a smart girl. I'm just usually juggling more lattes than my carrier can handle. And I know a lot of moms in the same coffee queue. Life happens—and sometimes my "oops" moments are material for a Thursday-night sitcom.

There was a time when I couldn't laugh at myself. Any type of tampon-on-the-floor moment would have sent me into a tailspin. I'd have felt like a failure, equating a simple mistake with a major character flaw. I'd cry and lay low, avoiding people or circumstances that might expose the real (imperfect) me. I actually got pretty good at controlling my environment, showcasing only competence. I was a prideful perfectionist so good at "the act" that I believed myself to be relatively pulled together.

"Never under any circumstances take a sleeping pill and a laxative on the same night." —DAVE BARRY

Then I had kids. The addition of these little variables to my life equation was a recipe for . . . health. That's right. Health. Not disaster. You see, with Peyton and Morgan in tow, "the act" fell apart. I tried to control it all but couldn't. And so, faced with the choice of learning to laugh at myself versus harboring resentment, anger and fear, I chose a life that is not always clean and perfect, but it's real, unpredictable and a whole lot more fun.

A Different Perspective

Learning to laugh at yourself is a life skill. It requires that you not take yourself too seriously, that you admit your flaws, acknowledge your mistakes and keep on living. It is actually quite scary to own up to your frailty and weakness, but it also gets others off the hook when you are honest about your own life.

I once received an email from a cousin, commenting on an article I'd written. She said, "Your stories are about how motherhood, marriage, friends, LIFE isn't easy, yet you always make us feel so much better by the end of the story, telling us we are normal and we'll survive. The funny thing is, I see you as a *Wonder Woman*, able to tackle so much and so well!"

After reading her comments, I thought: *She doesn't know me very well.*

I am no *Wonder Woman*, that's for sure. What I am is confident. I see myself as capable, and so I go for it—expecting success, knowing there may be mishaps along the way. I am not afraid to try new things nor afraid to fail. Life is so much more fun when I'm not trying to pull off the perfection façade. Some days I get my "ab" work-out just laughing. I laugh with others or at myself, relieving tension and anxiety, choosing to see the humor of life's speed bumps.

I'm learning to anticipate bumbles and mistakes. If I can avoid them, I do. But, unlike a sitcom, life is not scripted, and so the unexpected happens. The Big Lie is that everyone else has it more together. (And since life is one big competition, we can't let our guard down, right?) What a bunch of biscotti! Everyone I know and love makes mistakes. Their blunders endear them to me, affirming my own oversights and social gaffes.

"Knowing that we are loved unconditionally helps us laugh at ourselves when things don't go right—and when they do."

So laugh. Incorporate more humor into your life, even at your own expense. Victor Borge once said, "Laughter is the shortest distance between two people." This may be especially true with your children. Studies suggest that laughter is good for your health, boosting immunity[1] and possibly adding years to your life—just look at the longevity of Bob Hope and George Burns! What a bonus! Laughter is exercise for our bodies and our hearts; it lightens life and brings sweetness to ordinary moments.

A Cup of Humor

Of course, there are times when we really do want to crawl in a hole. It is nearly impossible to find the humor in a situation when we feel that it is a commentary on our essential character. This is where God comes in—unconditional love, no matter what. God's love endures forever (see Psalm 136:2). He created us for a special purpose. We all have different strengths, different weaknesses; Romans 12:6

says, "We have different gifts"—talents, skills, unique personality traits. What defines us is not what happens *to us*, but who we are and how we respond.

We are children of God! My confidence comes from that knowledge. Moving this truth from our heads to our hearts frees us to make mistakes, scatter tampons, fall in the mall, burn the garlic bread or spill the coffee. Knowing that we are loved unconditionally helps us laugh at ourselves when things don't go right—and when they do.

God has a perfect sense of humor, and He uses it wisely. He uses the hiccups of life to help keep us humble, to teach us and keep us focused on Him, not ourselves. Pride is public enemy number one, and life's laughable moments help give us perspective (see Proverbs 3:13 and 16:18).

I have a quote on my desk from an unknown author that says, "Angels can fly because they take themselves lightly." I bet angels laugh a lot. Angels know they are loved by God. Angels know who they are in God. Angels don't have anything to prove; they just are. We should aspire to be so rooted in God's love that we have a similar lightness of being. Now, there are some things you just can't giggle at; some mistakes—even unintentional ones—offend, hurt and destroy. This is when it is even more important to remember that we are loved by God, not on the basis of performance or works. Remember, God laughs with us, not at us.

When the blunders are basic, just laugh it off. Thank God for His love and give yourself the grace He's given you. (Read that sentence again.) He loves you—messes, spills, miscalculations and all. Now that's something to smile about.

Questions to STIR

1. When was the last time you laughed at your mistakes? Has it been too long? If so, think of a recent embarrassing moment or mistake you made. How did you react? What could you have done differently? In what ways can you employ laughter as a healthy response?

2. Do you buy into The Big Lie? Where do you discount yourself or feel the urge to compete? How does this affect your behavior, decisions and reactions to problems? Your sense of humor?

3. Is it hard for you to visualize God with a sense of humor? Do you think humor and godliness are compatible?

Soul Sip Solutions

1. List 10 ways you can incorporate more fun and laughter into your life. Watch a funny movie, buy silly glasses and wear them at dinner, or take a purple bubble bath with your toddler. Be imaginative. Try three things this week.

2. Look for an opportunity to laugh with your kids. Try to laugh at yourself, disarming a potentially embarrassing or tense situation. Help your children learn this skill as well.

3. Read Romans 5:1-5. What do these verses say to you about love, grace and acceptance? Pray and ask God to show you His heart for you and a specific application in your life.

Reflection and Challenge

What "Soul Sip Solution" did you try? How did it go? What did you learn? Record your thoughts. Pray and continue to become aware of the abundant humor in life. Practice laughing out loud several times a day (you might want to be by yourself, not in the middle of the grocery store, if you don't want someone to think you're crazy). Have "laugh sessions" with your kids to see how contagious it is.

COFFEE BREAK
WITH SARAH

Dear Moms,

I arrived late, which wasn't unusual, but then the preacher—a tall man with premature gray hair—called my name: "Sarah, where are you from?"

I looked up, startled, with the sudden awareness of all eyes on me, conspicuously in the spotlight, which was unusual for church. This, I thought, is either punishment for being late or a lesson to sit at the back of the church next Sunday. (Though when I sit in the back, I busy myself with the hairstyles of everyone in front of me instead of listening to the sermon.)

"Sarah," he repeated, "where are you from?"

I'm a frequent guest speaker at conferences. In fact, a few weeks prior, I had addressed a group of 450 and barely broke a sweat. But this morning . . . I froze.

Finally, I quietly answered, "I'm from Pace."

The preacher seemed puzzled by my brevity but continued with the morning announcements: "And, uh, that, folks, is one way to greet visitors."

What I had missed by being late was a discussion about welcoming newcomers. I had unknowingly been handpicked to act out an instructional skit.

"I'm sorry I put you on the spot," the preacher said later. "I thought you would be comfortable speaking up in front of the congregation."

"Well, you know that feeling of laughing at the worst possible time?" I said. "I thought when I opened my mouth that I would either laugh or curse, and either would have been totally inappropriate," I confessed.

"God loves you, Sarah. Always," he smiled and reassured me.

I had worried about being "appropriate" in church. I wanted my behavior to match the setting. Mostly, I didn't want to make a fool of myself. But failing to adroitly catch the ball tossed to me in a "think fast" fashion, I had fumbled.

I like to think that God had a good laugh at me that morning. For all my attempts at perfection, God knows my heart. He knows when I say the wrong thing, fall over my shoes or giggle at the large hat worn by the woman seated in the pew in front of me. And He loves me, you—all of us—anyway. Which is no laughing matter. And it's also why I'll be sitting in the very first pew again next Sunday.

Sarah Smiley

7

ALL WHIPPED UP

Support

✦—┆—✦

Call it a clan, call it a network, call it a tribe, call it a family:
Whatever you call it, whoever you are, you need one.
JANE HOWARD

For my yoke is easy and my burden is light.
MATTHEW 11:30

School project for Peyton. Playgroup for MoMo. Writing deadline. Community barbeque. Breakfast. Laundry. Grocery store. Call Heather. Check email. Reschedule dentist. Shave legs.

I am still in bed and my mind is already racing at light-speed, 0 to 60 things to do today. That's me. Nothing has characterized me so well since my eighth-grade addiction to Aqua Net hairspray.

 "Caffeine takes about 10 to 15 minutes to get into the blood-stream, and peak levels can be reached in 45 minutes, according to James D. Lane Ph.D., director of Duke University Medical Center Psychophysiology Laboratory." —LADIES HOME JOURNAL[1]

I tumble out of bed, pull on jeans and gulp coffee. I wake the kids, fix breakfast, pack lunches and check email.
Nourish yourself. Take time for Me.

I rush to the bus stop, power through the grocery store, bank, post office, dry cleaners. I go to playgroup with my toddler, gobble half her Happy Meal (with an extra-large diet soda), then speed home to put her down for a nap. Once she's snoozing, my mind races. I have an hour—what should I do next?

Take care of yourself. Take time for Me.

I grab a cup of green tea and scramble to my computer, frantic to finish an article. The phone rings and I console a teary friend. My little one wakes. I grab her, fix a snack and sit down to pay bills. Frustration wells up; I am so busy, yet I have nothing tangible to show for my day. I scan my to-do list. I am a gummy bear caught in a sweaty fist. Tension presses on my shoulders. How can I ever keep up?

Set priorities. Put Me first. Don't try to do it all.

The rest of my afternoon is filled with carpool, supper, helping with homework and playing referee to sibling squabbles. After dinner, my children want to play, but I don't take the time; after baths, I tuck them into bed. Once they're asleep, I do dishes and a load of laundry, and then rush back to my computer and the impending deadline.

Take time for Me.

"Take time for me."

What? I look around. No one is there. Am I am losing it?

"Honey," a voice calls again. "I haven't seen you all day. Come sit with me."

Sit? While I would love to relax with my husband, this deadline hangs over me like a career noose.

"Okay, as soon as I'm done," I reply, knowing he'll be asleep by the time I finish.

Hours later, I wilt into bed like sandwich lettuce in the sun, feeling guilty that I haven't played with my kids, connected with my husband or exercised. I don't know how to keep up, but I figure I'll try again tomorrow.

A Weak Spot in the Bridge

On August 1, 2007, the eight-lane I-35 Mississippi River Bridge collapsed in Minnesota.[2] The bridge gave way during the evening rush hour, sending cars plummeting into the river below. Why did it fail?

Was it lack of maintenance? Did a key support buckle? As of this writing, no one is quite sure why it collapsed, but one thing is sure: it had more stress than it could take on that fateful summer day.

As moms, we are like bridges. We carry heavy loads—and like the I-35 bridge, sometimes we experience more stress than we can handle. I've never met a mom who didn't have something to do; we all carry a lot of responsibility. The problem is, when we are unduly stressed, we can fail. A neglect of self-maintenance may cause us to lose focus, to worry, to deliver mediocre results or develop a melancholy, even critical attitude toward ourselves and others. We may suffer a weakened immune system, illness, fatigue, depression or complete collapse.

Moms who are in spiritual, physical and emotional balance, however, are seemingly enthusiastic, inspiring "Super Moms." They are productive problem-solvers, quick on their feet, and they (usually) don't burn dinner. I have "Super Mom" days when I feel sturdy and strong, so I pile on the "cars" of responsibility and obligation, optimistic that I can hold it all, coping with any stress. Then days, or perhaps even hours later, overwhelmed and overloaded, like the I-35 bridge, I'll crash to the ground. Even when I am careful about prioritization and saying no to unnecessary commitments, life happens. Those caffeine-fueled days when I forget God, don't play with my kids or connect with my husband actually weaken my "bridge." I need support. All moms, especially in today's world, need support—and lots of it. Acknowledging that we need help does not make us weak; it makes us human.

Building a Foundation

The secret of "Super Mom" success is a strong foundation of support. So how do we build this foundation? What contributes to the health of our bridge, so to speak? How do we get there?

For me, personal support starts with a network of family and friends. It's key to have people to talk with, laugh with and confide in—who will also watch my kids on short notice if needed. I have writer friends who support my career as a wordsmith, reading my material and providing feedback. Other helpful services (when I can afford them) include: the dry cleaners (so I don't have to iron), a hairdresser (so I can stay blonde), prepackaged dinners (so I don't have to plan menus) and a housekeeper (so I don't have to scrub grout). I realize that resources for this type of support may be limited, necessitating a tradeoff, but the ability to offload lesser responsibilities frees me for gainful employment, creative endeavors and time with my children.

☕ *"Many parents now live with a precariousness that keeps them constantly on edge. It makes them anxious. It sometimes makes them feel ashamed. It can make them feel like failures."*

—JUDITH WARNER, *PERFECT MADNESS: MOTHERHOOD IN THE AGE OF ANXIETY*[3]

I am thankful for a roof over my head, reliable transportation, a home office, my church, our children's schools and other physical structures that strengthen my ability to be efficient and effective. My husband is amazingly supportive in sharing the workload as well. His commitment, love and involvement in parenting are integral to me keeping up with all I do.

All these supports—from people and services to strategic thinking and planning—help us moms spend our time where it matters most. For example: Regular exercise is important for stress management and overall health, but how many of us take the time? Whether we arrange for a babysitter so that we can get to the gym, hire a personal trainer to come to our home or develop a workout system with our kids, support means finding a way to break a sweat! Proper support ensures that we have time to rest, to breathe, to give our best to what matters. Otherwise, we are just droids going through the motions, missing what life is meant to be.

A Cup of Support

The most critical support of all is spiritual support. God provides us with the Ultimate Support: Jesus. Paul, an early follower of Jesus, reminds us that "[We] can do everything through [Jesus] who gives [us] strength" (Philippians 4:13). God created all things (see Genesis 1); He created the seasons, bringing balance to nature—and He can bring balance to our lives.

In my to-do story, God's voice was urging me to take time for Him. As the checklist started to tick through my brain, I should have closed my eyes and given the whole list to Jesus—seeking guidance for my day and an internal place of rest amidst my busy agenda. Starting the day with prayer and a simple devotional makes the day less harried and reminds us of what matters most. This infusion of affirmation and truth at the beginning of the day is like installing steel girders in the structure of my being; I am strengthened for whatever weight (stress) I may need to bear. God sustains all things by His powerful word (see Hebrews 1:3).

Moms need support. A lot is expected of us—and we can't do it alone. Show me a "Super Mom" and I'll show you a solid support system. Got to have it! And it is Jesus who is the indestructible foundation poised under our interstate, preventing us from collapse, keeping our "bridge" in perfect balance. He is, indeed, the Ultimate Support.

Questions to STIR

1. What weight/stress can you unload? Do you ever feel like your bridge is going to collapse? In what areas of your life could you use support?

2. Do you take quiet time for Jesus each day, or do you rush into the morning without His infusion of peace and support? How can you adjust your schedule to make Jesus a priority?

3. What are some of your successes? Stresses? In what ways can you look to God for support in your day-to-day life?

Soul Sip Solutions

1. List the areas of your life in which you might benefit from support. Brainstorm possibilities and action steps to get help in each area. Pray for God to guide your life and bring an infusion of support.

2. Pick two key areas from Question 1 in which you need support. Pick one that you can control, and make it happen. Second, pick one that only God can control, and continue to pray for the support you need.

3. If you are not a member of a local church, over the next month make it a priority to visit a few. Go to their websites and read any newsletters or material available on their programs. How might you plug into a community of godly support?

Reflection and Challenge

List all your negative stressors (looming deadlines, child discipline issues, misplaced keys). Brainstorm ways to incorporate more "positive" stress (shopping for a gift, exercising at the gym, clearing your calendar for a vacation). What defines support for you? What foundation is your bridge built upon? Read Matthew 7:24-27.

8

CAUTION: HOT!

Self-control

Anger is one letter short of danger.
AUTHOR UNKNOWN

The LORD is compassionate and gracious, slow to anger, abounding in love.
PSALM 103:8

"You have 20 minutes until the school bus comes, Peyton. Is your backpack ready to go?" I yell from the kitchen, where I sip my morning coffee.

No response.

"Hey, Peyton," I holler again. "Is your stuff ready? Let's go! You need to eat breakfast before the bus comes."

No response.

"Peyton?!" I put down my coffee and march upstairs to her room. She is sitting on her bed, oblivious, fiddling with a new birthday toy. Clothes, books and toys blanket the floor like winter snow. I pick my way through the disarray, strategically stepping toward her like a hiker stepping on rocks to cross a river.

"Hey, Peyton," I say, my face now just inches from hers. "Ready for breakfast?"

"Oh," she says, looking up for the first time. "Sure."

"Well grab your backpack and come down to the kitchen. What do you want? Oatmeal or eggs?"

"Eggs."

"Okay." I return downstairs and start the range. A few minutes later, Peyton appears, looking tentative and guilty, as if she's just flushed my wedding ring down the toilet.

"I forgot . . . I have homework."

"You *had* homework?" I clarify, a sharp edge to my voice. "I asked you last night if you had any, and you said no."

"I forgot."

"You forgot? Are you kidding me?" I look at the clock. Sixteen minutes until the bus. "Well, what did you have to do?"

"Math pages."

Great. Math pages. Peyton's most difficult subject.

"Well, sit down and start doing them."

Peyton dutifully sits down at the counter but doesn't move. "I need a pencil."

"What do you mean you need a pencil?" I ask, getting more irritated. "Don't you have one in your backpack? You have like 40,000 pencils! Why don't you have one when you need it?"

"I dunno." Her eyes are downcast; she is suddenly very interested in the pattern of the granite countertop. She doesn't budge.

"Get a pencil!" I say, my words exploding out of my mouth.

She startles and scrambles to my office. I follow her, hands on hips, watching. She opens the cabinet and takes out my carrier of writing instruments.

"Oh, no you don't," I say before she can grab one. "You need to get one of your own. You lose mine."

"But I don't know where any of my pencils are," she says in a desperate whine.

"That's because your room is such a mess! If you kept your room organized, you'd know where to find something when you need it!"

▯ *If you feel yourself starting to lose it:*
Walk away. Breathe. Do push-ups. Pray.

The morning tension escalates. Peyton misses the bus and eats a cereal bar in the car as I drive her to school, lecturing her the whole way. Her school snack is a last-minute granola bar pulled from the glove compartment. She finishes her math pages but cries while doing them. She is late for school.

When I get back to the car after signing her into class, my angry soapbox morphs into suffocating bubbles of shame. I rest my head on the steering wheel and weep.

You've *Got* to Be Kidding Me!

Believe it or not, I never knew I could even *get* angry until I had children. Sure I'd been upset—about a bad grade or hurt feelings—but I never realized I was capable of spontaneous combustion until I became a mom. It is so weird. My ability to go from June Cleaver to Cruella DeVil is terrifying. And humbling. I can go days, even weeks, with a patient, cheerful countenance, and then anger sneaks up on me, silently, stealthily; in an instant it consumes me, shaking the foundations of my very being.

A deep breath and an inch of perspective would have reminded me that no homework assignment is worth a tearful, frustrated morning for my daughter (or me). I could have said, "What a bummer. I hope you don't get in trouble for not completing your math pages." I could have sent a note to the teacher. I could have been more generous with my pencils, remembering that lessons on organization are not best taught 10 minutes before the school bus. Even as I was reacting that morning, I knew that anger was not the answer, but I was Dorothy in the whirlwind, not sure how to get out of the storm.

Anger is an accumulation of fear, hidden hurts and past disappointments. We all have different triggers; for me, feelings of anger often surface when I feel frustrated or sense a loss of control. For someone else, a trigger might be being lied to or not taken seriously. Whatever the provocation, being a mom is apt to light us up like a fuse on the Fourth of July. Our children can bring out the very best in us, revealing depths of love and creativity we never knew existed. But along with the good may come unresolved issues and fears.

We must work through them, or like the juice in a baking apple pie that looks pleasing and sweet, we can bubble up spontaneously, burning those closest to us with destructive splatters of fury.

Proactive Versus Reactive

Anger can snap in us like an osteoporotic bone, like a winning streak come to an end or a PEZ dispenser in demand. It can destroy the foundations of the very life we aspire to if we do not proactively seek solutions and ways to manage our frustrations, irritations and fears.

The first step in this process is awareness. When we are over-tired, hungry, super-stressed or nearing *that* time of the month, we are likely to be "set off" much more easily. Be aware of this and proceed with caution. When we feel the bonds that hold us together vibrating like a snare drum, we can take a step back, refocus and make an intentional choice to respond appropriately.

A second important step is recognizing our triggers and working to avoid them. If we know that a messy house makes us crazy, then when laundry is littered across the bedroom, it might be a great time to have the kids help tidy, or hire a housekeeper. If your trigger is fear of kidnapping, and your children love to hide in the clothes rounders at the mall, you might take a friend shopping with you to help keep an eye on the little ones, or hire a sitter. Carefully consider what stirs your anger soup, and take steps to avoid those situations.

Third, when we do feel apt to snap like a ginger cookie, we must learn to direct our energy in more positive directions. No yelling like Judge Judy. Step away. Breathe. Go for a walk. Do push-ups. (The push-up thing really works for me, as many times I can't just leave the house for a cool-down stroll, and push-ups require enough energy that my anger is deflated like a post-party balloon.) Time taken to gain some perspective in a situation is time well spent, because most all things can be resolved without an angry reaction, which usually just compounds the problem.

Of course, we all have our baggage, whether it's Louis Vuitton, Coach or Samsonite, and some issues are classics that never get old. If you feel that anger is a recurrent theme in your life, or unusually problematic, seek the advice of a counselor or therapist. Also seek the transformation and self-control we can only get through the restorative love of Jesus.

A Cup of Self-control

"Therefore, prepare your minds for action; be self-controlled; set your hope fully on the grace to be given you" (1 Peter 1:13). We need to prepare our minds and be disciplined and purposeful about our thoughts and actions, avoiding anger to the best of our ability. Still, no matter how controlled or "good" we may be, we are plagued by our human nature. There is no way we can make it without God's grace.

My friend Penny says that if she could take her own advice, life would be great. The only problem is, living out the things we know to be right, consistently and without error, is a tough order. Even when we feel that we are making the right decisions, *our way* may not truly be *the* way; there is only one right, true way, and that is Jesus (see John 14:6).

God's divine nature gives us an example to follow. He is compassionate and gracious, *slow to anger*, and abounding in love (see Exodus 34:6). The first step toward transformation is admitting our anger and surrendering all to Him: the fears, frustrations, irritations, disappointments, worry . . . all the stuff. Ask forgiveness and invite God into every area of your life. Hold nothing back; there is forgiveness and grace for every detail.

Next, accept responsibility: You may not always be in control of outcomes, but you are in charge of your actions and reactions. Model your life after Jesus. Jesus trusted God with His life. He spoke the truth and abounded in love. I wasn't exactly "abounding in love" when I was yelling at my daughter. Perhaps if I'd taken a minute to do some push-ups and look to Jesus (spiritual push-ups), my response would have been different.

Much of what we do and don't do, say and don't say, act and react will contribute to how our children "see" the world and themselves.

God, through the Holy Spirit, gives us the power to act rightly (see Luke 12:12; Acts 1:8; 1 Corinthians 3:16; 1 Corinthians 12–13).

Galatians 5:22-23 says, "the fruit of the Spirit is love, joy, peace, patience, kindness, goodness, faithfulness, gentleness, and self-control." Translation? When we are walking with God, looking to Him for direction, and empowered by the Holy Spirit, we have the ability to overcome anger and manifest the very qualities of God.

Who couldn't use more love, peace and patience in her life? Who wouldn't appreciate an infusion of gentleness and self-control? I know when I became a mom, the stakes got much higher. I am now not only responsible for figuring out my own life, but for guiding my two daughters. Much of what I do and don't do, say and don't say, act and react, will contribute to how they "see" themselves and the world. I can choose to do it my way—and see what happens—or look to Jesus for a divine example and the power to overcome fear, disappointments, frustrations and anger.

When I am walking with Jesus and really seeking His heart, I don't very often get angry. I am a gentle and loving mom. Though when I fail, I never encounter an angry God. There is always grace for me. Now *that* is an example worth following!

Questions to STIR

1.   Think of the last time you got angry. What were the triggers? How can you avoid these in the future? What steps can you take to proactively eliminate some of these triggers from your life entirely?

2.   When you yell at your kids, what message does that send? How can you communicate love, even in tough situations, when you may well have a right to be angry?

3.   Look up these verses: Exodus 34:6; Numbers 14:1; and Psalms 86:15; 103:8 and 145:8. What do these verses say about the nature of God?

Soul Sip Solutions

1.   Take some time to write down some instances in which anger got the best of you. How could you have reacted differently?

List five things you can do next time you feel yourself start to get angry. Post the list in a prominent place (fridge, bathroom mirror) to remind you.

2. Is there a recent situation in which you yelled or reacted inappropriately in anger? Pray and ask God to forgive you. Then go to the person you have hurt, apologize and ask that person's forgiveness as well.

3. Read 2 Peter 1:5-6. What does it mean to "make every effort"? How can you make every effort in these areas and what might that look like? List some ways that you can "make every effort" toward self-control.

Reflection and Challenge

During the next week, take some additional time to read and work through the "Questions to STIR" and the "Soul Sip Solutions." How have these exercises changed your perspective on anger? Do you see yourself as able to be self-controlled through the power of the Holy Spirit? Why or why not?

_____

_____

_____

_____

_____

_____

_____

_____

_____

_____

9

WHAT DID *SHE* ORDER?

Satisfaction

In jealousy there is more self-love than love.
FRANÇOIS, DUC DE LA ROCHEFOUCAULD, *MAXIMS*, 1665

A heart at peace gives life to the body, but envy rots the bones.
PROVERBS 14:30

I had the afternoon to myself. My husband had taken our daughters to a rugby game, and I was left with a few hours on my own. I was not immediately sure what to do with this rare gift. My mind vacillated: Sleep? *No.* Exercise? *Nah.* Paperwork? *Boring.* A movie? *Nope.* A manicure? *Maybe.* The mall? *Might be fun without an entourage in the dressing room.* I wasted precious minutes sorting through my choices. Finally, I decided to snuggle up on the couch and read for a few minutes—then zip over to the mall.

Two pages into my book, I was in dreamland. I bolted awake an hour later, refreshed, but angry I'd snoozed away part of my Saturday. Had I missed my mall window? I looked at the clock. I still had time, so I grabbed my purse and headed out the door.

Once at the mall, I bought some lemonade, then headed straight for my favorite store. Soon, I was sipping and shopping, having a fabulous time browsing the racks. Then I saw her.

She was an acquaintance from the neighborhood, looking as if she'd just stepped off the pages of *Vogue.* Her make-up, nails and hair were perfect—and she was sipping a Venti-size Starbucks. I looked down at my shorts and flip-flops. I hadn't taken time to change out of my weekend grubbies. My nails were in severe need of attention, and my lemonade was instantly second rate. *What kind of coffee is she drinking?* I wondered, eyeing the telltale black markings on her cup.

"Hi, Ella," I said. "How are you?" She looked up, found me and smiled.

"Hi, there," she replied, giving me a head-to-toe once-over. "Nice to see you. Whatcha shopping for?"

"Oh, maybe some jeans," I said, uncomfortably. "You?"

"I'm just window-shopping."

"Cool. Well, nice to see you," I said. "I'm off to the GAP."

"See you."

As I walked away, I felt my face flush. I wished I'd looked better, had her hair, her nails, even her outfit. I wanted her coffee too. And I was on my way to get it. I dropped my lemonade in the nearest trash and made my way to get a little bit of *what she had.*

"By age 3, a child begins to experience 'evaluative embarrassment.' More than just realizing that all eyes are on her, she'll size herself up based on social rules or standards and others' scrutiny."

—JULIE ROSE, *WONDERTIME*[1]

An Empty Cup

It is so easy to fall prey to jealousy. The second I saw my neighbor, I failed to see the abundance in my own life. The luxurious afternoon, the "me" time, the refreshing lemonade, every bit of it was eclipsed by my distorted perception that what she had—how she looked, what she was wearing, even her drink—was better. The encounter took me from a place of bliss to twitter and torment. The peace of the day was ruined.

Jealousy. It's yucky stuff. It murks about in one's mind, comparing, weighing, measuring, judging. It suffocates gratitude. Someone who is jealous of another is failing to see her own blessings, talents and worth. I am usually not jealous; I'm confident in my abilities, my appearance, my worth—except when it comes to this woman. For some reason, she always seems to have it pulled together just a little bit more: She wears the season's cutest shoes, her hair is smooth and styled (while mine seems frizzy); even her Christmas cards seem especially creative. Entertaining the thought that she has it all—with no problems—is truly naïve. We all have strengths and weaknesses. My jealousy of her relegates me to the ranks of an immature, insecure teen—someone who hasn't learned to see her own worth.

Dumping Out the Dregs

Have you ever made coffee when the filter caves in and the grounds get mixed in with the whole pot, leaving a dark sediment at the bottom of each cup (and sometimes in your teeth)? Just as those dregs ruin our morning brew, jealousy darkens our spirit and taints our perspective.

The first step in clearing the dregs is embracing the truth that no one is perfect (see Romans 3:23) and we are all created with different gifts (see Romans 12:6). These are two important, grounding truths. While Ella may look fabulous, and her Christmas cards seem better, it doesn't matter. Different talents, different strengths; no need to compare. (A total aside—but considering the true meaning of Christmas, why am I even comparing Christmas cards, anyway?)

My friend Karen has a great eye for interior design. Her house is immaculate. She teaches yoga, runs a business and is an amazing cook. She knows what she likes, what her strengths are, and spends her time pursuing the activities—and life—best suited to her. Recently, I asked her if she played golf. She said no.

"You should learn," I said. "You'd be great."

"No, I shouldn't learn," she said, matter-of-factly. "I don't want to. I am busy enough doing the things I love and am good at. I don't need to learn golf. Everything doesn't have to be my thing."

Her words sunk into my heart like an anchor. You know, my house isn't as fashionable as Karen's, my meals aren't as tasty and I've taken yoga twice, both times straining muscles I didn't know existed. And I'm okay with that. You know why? Because I like golf, writing and photography. I have different interests, different strengths. I would rather play a quick nine holes with my husband after work and grab a burger on the way home than spend the time trying to cook a gourmet meal. My life fits me. Karen's life fits her. Ella's fits her. Life is not a competition. Accepting each person as created equally with different gifts and talents opens the door for a richer appreciation of self and others. It fills our cups with gratitude and satisfaction.

A Cup of Satisfaction

Imagine a world in which we all know our worth. Think how different the world would be. Ecclesiastes 4:4 says envy is "meaningless, a chasing after the wind." And yet, we do chase the wind. You can't turn on a television, much less turn a corner, without being bombarded with the marketing message: more is better . . . and makes us better. But how much do we need?

Focusing on what we don't have keeps us in a straitjacket of want.

A few years ago, after the tsunami rocked Southeast Asia, I traveled to India on a missions trip. What I encountered changed me forever; I came home with a new appreciation for my life and all I have. I saw people living in shacks—with no shoes, no health care, no food. These people had *nothing,* by our standards, and yet they were so gracious and grateful. I began to see that having too much can keep us captive to a "more" mentality. Though the "I want" mindset is easy to succumb to, it blinds us to our blessings.

When we accept our value in God and take time each day to express gratitude *for what we have,* peace comes. Satisfaction comes. Focusing on what we don't have keeps us in the straitjacket of want.

This is tough stuff. We live in a competitive culture. I feel jealous more than I care to admit. Taking stock of my life, and choosing to appreciate how God has blessed me, opens my heart to gratitude. It doesn't take long for satisfaction to pour in. It is a heavenly brew, filling my cup to the brim.

Questions to STIR

1. Think of a time when you felt jealous of another person. What triggered it?

2. What are your gifts, strengths and talents? Where do you feel you lack or don't measure up?

3. Look up Proverbs 23:17. What does it mean to be "zealous for the Lord"? How can you turn from the sin of jealousy?

Soul Sip Solutions

1. Bust out the paper again. List 50 things you are thankful for. Pray and thank God now. If you can't think of 50 items, ask Him to show you the blessings in your life.

2. Find a couple of local organizations that help the needy. In the next month, arrange to volunteer a couple of hours. Journal about how this experience changes you.

3. Think of someone you have been jealous of in the past and still have contact with. In the next two weeks, use your talents to bless that person: Write her a note, bake some cookies, take a great photograph of her, and so forth.

Reflection and Challenge

How'd it go? Did you complete the Soul Sip Solutions? Why or why not? If yes, what was your experience? Pray and ask God to help you see your blessings each day, in every moment.

_____

_____

_____

_____

_____

_____

10

A CUP OF SILENCE

Solitude

We live in a very tense society. We are pulled apart . . .
and we all need to learn how to pull ourselves together. . . .
I think that at least part of the answer lies in solitude.
HELEN HAYES

I have no peace, no quietness; I have no rest, but only turmoil.
JOB 3:26

I rise in the quiet stillness of dawn. As soon as my foot sneaks out
of the blankets, our Labrador, Trapper, is by the bedside, greeting
me, licking my toes. We walk downstairs together; I stumble, still
groggy with slumber; he dances with excitement, a Tigger-like
spring propelling him down the steps to his food bowl. As we step
into the kitchen, the tappity-tap of his toenails on the hardwood is
the only sound that breaks the early repose.

A pinky-orange sunrise romances me—a background of pine
trees and three deer walking through our yard add to the splendor.
I start the coffee, grab my Bible and make my way to the couch, my
favorite morning spot. I snuggle in and listen. Trapper has eaten
and gone back to bed. Now, the quiet hum of the heater, an occa-
sional passing car and the percolating coffeemaker are the only
traitors to the silence.

God is in these moments. In the still mornings, I can feel His
presence. Waking to a sweet tangerine sky—painted by our Creator—is worth my daily battle with an angry alarm clock and the
cozy comforter that tries to keep me captive. I love this time.

What better way to greet the day than surrounded by beauty, encouraged by God's word and blessed by the silence—while taking roasty-warm sips of an organic, full-bodied coffee. It is the perfect date with God.

I'll admit it. Sometimes it's really, really hard to get up, especially when the seasons change. With clocks now adjusted to daylight savings, I awake to pitch-blackness. Trapper laps my toes, telling me it's time for breakfast, but I don't believe him. I turn over, wanting to stay in the tenebrous toastiness. But alas, the alarm clock doesn't lie, and minutes later jolts me to reality.

If I linger too long—or hit snooze once too often—I miss it all. The precious time is lost. The serenity of silence and the sherbet sky are gone. The traffic on the road picks up, my girls wake and the morning's agenda jumps at me like an army of disoriented grasshoppers. The cacophony of the day sings a chorus too loud to ignore, and so, more than anything, I treasure my morning moments all the more.

"I've long since stopped feeling guilty about taking 'being' time; it's something we all need for our spiritual health, and often we don't take enough of it."

—MADELEINE L'ENGLE, *WALKING ON WATER: REFLECTIONS ON FAITH AND ART*[1]

Alone Time

It is hard to find solitude in today's world. Like me, most moms rush from dawn to dusk, checking off to-do lists, shuffling kids and playing "Beat the Clock" with their speedometers pegged. However, it is only when we slow down and find focus in quiet moments of solitude that we can clearly see the road ahead. In her book *Simple Abundance*, Sarah Ban Breathnach says, "Usually, when the distractions of daily life deplete our energy, the first thing we eliminate is the thing we need the most: quiet, reflective time. Time to dream, time to think, time to contemplate what's working and what's not so we can make changes for the better."[2] Ladies, we need this time. When we take time to pray, reflect and *just be,* we are better equipped to deal with the detours and speed bumps of life. When we employ and embrace a regular practice of solitude, our perspective is altogether different and life is much more enjoyable. Solitude is essential. This quiet provides a time for reflection—and like a natural spring that continually gives, solitude is mom-nurturing.

The Quiet Benefits

Solitude can also be scary. I have a friend who doesn't like to be alone—she even makes dates to grocery shop, when she can arrange it. She is a very gregarious, outgoing woman, but I sometimes wonder if she is afraid of the quiet.

Alone time is an opportunity for inspiration and introspection. For me, solitude fuels creativity; I am often inspired by something I've read in these moments, and the application of the thought or lesson brings me great joy. But for many, the look inward may trigger anxiety. Introspection is a step toward self-awareness, self-analysis and self-discovery. If you don't like what you see, or have personal issues to work through (who doesn't?), solitude gives you the opportunity to confront them.

During my morning quiet times, I usually read my Bible or a devotional, and I pray. When I can carve out other "me" time, I often read, daydream, doodle, write, sing or meditate. My friend Roxane says, "Thank goodness it takes three hours to get my hair done, because this alone time is a huge treat!" Another friend finds solitude in the car, while driving alone. There is no right or wrong way to be in solitude—you just need to find it, have it, experience it.

Moms usually need to schedule solitude. You need to make it work. While your kids are napping, pick a spot that stirs your soul and insist that others honor this time. And honor it yourself—every day. Turn off the TV and radio; silence all the phones. Consider it purposeful preoccupation, a daily mini-getaway designed to help you get acquainted with yourself—and God.

Consider this quote from Henry David Thoreau: "I went to the woods because I wished to live deliberately, to front only the essential facts of life, and see if I could not learn what it had to teach, and not, when I came to die, discover that I had not lived." How might deliberate solitude help us live better?

☕ *"God wants us to follow Him daily, not follow a plan."*

—HENRY T. BLACKABY AND CLAUDE V. KING,
EXPERIENCING GOD: KNOWING AND DOING HIS WILL[3]

A Cup of Solitude

Life is meant to be enjoyed; each day is our red carpet opportunity to shine. Remember, Jesus came so that we might have life and have it to the full—but a full schedule does not necessarily make a full life. Take time for solitude—and during this time alone, seek Jesus.

Matthew 6:25-34 tells us that when we put God first, He takes care of all the details: what we eat, what we wear, all the worries of life. There is a lot we could worry about, but building into our lives peaceful moments when we can commune with God guarantees we won't carry our burdens alone.

When Jesus was on earth, He withdrew into solitude on a regular basis: "Very early in the morning, while it was still dark, Jesus got up, left the house and went off to a solitary place, where He prayed" (Mark 1:35); "But Jesus often withdrew to lonely places and prayed" (Luke 5:16); "At daybreak Jesus went out to a solitary place" (Luke 4:42); He modeled the communion with God that is so essential to our spiritual growth and overall wellbeing. No doubt, these times alone provided focus and refreshment—and if Jesus recognized the need for it, shouldn't we?

In her book *I Married Adventure*, Luci Swindoll reflects on the average busy person: "I know few people who take adequate time for reflection—and many who regret they don't. Who said, 'The important always gets sacrificed on the altar of the urgent'? Taking time is a better way to live."[4]

Amen, sister! You can say that again—well, actually, don't. Let's just enjoy the silence.

Questions to STIR

1. Is your life so "loud" that you cannot (or do not take the time to) hear God? How can you build solitude into your life?

2. Read Matthew 11:28-30. What does this say to you about rest and refreshment through Jesus?

3. Reread Matthew 6:33. What would it look like for you to seek God first in every area of your life? What difference do you think it would make?

Soul Sip Solutions

1. If you do not have a place that "stirs your soul," create one. Find a comfy corner of your home, then add your Bible, a potted flower and a few simple things that you love to the space.

2. If you do not already have a time of solitude, try to schedule a few times this week. Consider a morning coffee date with God, before the day's distractions disrupt your intentions for quiet time.

3. Go for a walk by yourself. (Don't bring your iPod.) Just relax and revel in this time alone with God.

Reflection and Challenge

Did you find solitude this week? What have you learned about yourself? About God? Did you have any creative inspirations? Write down a few of your thoughts.

_____

_____

_____

_____

_____

_____

COFFEE BREAK
WITH JOY

Dear Girls,

I just got back from enjoying coffee on the beach. Life has been so busy lately, the quiet was a treat. I really got in touch with how I miss my quiet times when busyness takes over . . . and how I miss you!

Taking time out is like making a date with myself and God. I can hear myself again . . . and sometimes even hear a God-thought!

I still take long walks like I always did when you girls were young. It's my time to "walk away" from all that is happening. Sometimes you just gotta "Stop and Walk!"

This morning, I was thinking about how fun it's been that you both have "caught" my fondness for cooking, good books and puppies! And how I would love for you both to find a place of solitude and quiet in your busy lives. I am so proud of you both . . . and pray that your lives are rich with friends, family . . . and an understanding of yourselves and the God who made you.

"Stop, Look, and Listen" are far more than street crossing instructions! They are excellent words for life:

Stop the busyness for a moment.

Look around you. Savor where God has placed you. Where you are is no accident.

Listen to yourself . . . to your surroundings . . . and listen for God. Ask Him to tell you all He has for you. Create a space to hear it.

You guys are the best!

I love you,
XXOO Mom
(Joy Lehman)

11

YOUR OWN
SPECIAL BLEND

Purpose

The purpose of life is a life of purpose.
ROBERT BYRNE

And we know that in all things God works for the good of those who love him,
who have been called according to his purpose.
ROMANS 8:28

"How are things going?" I asked my friend Josie one morning over coffee.

"Great," she replied. "I'm just busy helping with PTO, volunteering in my kids' classrooms and leading the Girl Scout troop again this year."

"Wow, that's a lot. What do you do for yourself?"

"I don't," she confessed. "In fact, when my kids graduate, I'm not sure what I'll do." A look of consternation kidnapped her smile.

"Aw, come on," I said. "You're smart. You're good at a lot of things."

"I'm good at decorating for school parties and making team spaghetti dinners," she said with a sigh, "but I'm not sure those skills will be helpful once my kids are out of the house."

As we talked, it became evident that not only did my friend define herself solely through her role as a mother, but she also lacked an overall sense of purpose outside of parenting. When her children moved on to college—and started their own lives—she believed hers would be over in some respects. She had always wanted to be a mom, and loved it, but dreaded the day her children would not "need" her as much. I tried to encourage Josie, but in the end, we both left the coffee shop that day with heavy hearts; she was missing the proverbial big picture.

Knowing Who You Are

I have other friends who feel like Josie. Many of my mom-friends, especially those who stay at home, define themselves exclusively through their role as a parent—as if they are mama kangaroos who only see their value in toting a little joey. These are great women, fantastic moms; yet, when they are honest, many reveal an overall lack of vision and purpose outside of being a mom. I also have friends who lack a sense of purpose beyond their careers. They tie their worth and value to a paycheck or accolades. Both groups see themselves as one-dimensional caterpillars, unaware they are meant to become glorious butterflies.

Purpose gives meaning and direction to our lives—bringing fulfillment in even mundane tasks. Purpose is not what we do; it is the driving force behind our actions. It is NOT being PTA president, a great volunteer, a fantastic employee, championing a cause, or even being a mom. Defining ourselves by activities, titles or things limits the scope of all God wants for us.

"For most of us, the most powerful sense of meaning comes from doing something that makes us feel as if we're making a contribution to the world."

—LORETTA LaROCHE, *LIFE IS SHORT—WEAR YOUR PARTY PANTS*[1]

I used to be a corporate junkie. When I left my career to stay home with our daughter, Peyton, I felt conflicted; if I couldn't make money, what did I have to offer? I didn't know my purpose. I turned to God, and He began to change my point of view. I spent a lot of time in prayer, seeking God's heart. I wrote down the things I liked and was good at and tried different activities. Being a mom to Peyton topped the list; writing, encouraging friends and taking pictures were also on the list—but all these things were only a part of my purpose.

The underlying theme of love began to emerge: Love God, love my family and love others with all that I am; and use my life to bless others. I finally came to understand these things: Heavenly purpose is perspective; we are a conduit for God's love. Purpose is God's *personalized* service to others through us, taking the hugeness of God's love and pinpointing it in our own uniqueness. Purpose is the practical application of love.

Sharing Who You Are

Sometimes we get so involved in making purpose such a complicated and mysterious thing that we lose sight of the fact that we are in the process of living it. You've heard it said: Grow where you're planted—or transplanted, for that matter. God uses us right where we are. When I am in line with God's heart, everything I do falls under the umbrella of my purpose: mothering, writing, worship, career, relationships—it all rolls in. I experience extreme satisfaction when I can use my talents and gifts to bless others. I know my life has meaning—eternal meaning.

It's easy to get it into our heads that we are not up to the task and wonder: Can I do *that*? Will I be good enough? Then a quiet voice inside me says, "Try. I am with you" (see Isaiah 41:10). We often think we must do something big to really make a difference, but I've discovered that it is not always the big things that matter most; simple acts create a legacy of meaning. Marian Wright Edelman said, "We must not, in trying to think about how we can make a difference, ignore the small daily differences we can make, which, over time, add up to big differences we cannot foresee."

I am consistent in reading with my kids at bedtime. I give great hugs. I make a mean grilled cheese. I felt empty when leaving the corporate job, but more time with my family is incredibly important and gives my life fullness. Long after the corporate "bottom line" is forgotten, my investment in my daughters will be compounding exponentially. The little details, especially with children, add up to huge dividends.

Josie is a great caregiver, a terrific organizer. Perhaps when her children go off to college, she'll help run a rescue mission, or volunteer in a grade school. In simple acts of love that make a profound difference, Josie would continue to find meaning—understanding that her purpose is just being herself to the fullest.

A Cup of Purpose

Just like a bellybutton, we all have a purpose. Ephesians 2:10 tells us, "For we are God's workmanship, created in Christ Jesus to do good works, which God prepared in advance for us to do." God can't steer a parked car, but when we begin moving, God directs us to the life He has for us, the life we were meant to live.

> *"For it is God who works in you to will and act according to His good purpose."* —PHILIPPIANS 2:13

Proverbs 19:21 states, "Many are the plans in a [woman's] heart, but it is the LORD's purpose that prevails." A life lacking true purpose, or centered around our own ambitions, eventually feels empty. Helen Keller, whose life is a testimony to us all, once said, "Many people have a wrong idea of what constitutes true happiness. It is not attained through self-gratification, but through fidelity to a worthy purpose."

Ask God how you might more fully live in what He has called you to. If you seek meaning for your life, ask Him to reveal it to you. God works in each of us in accordance with His purpose for our lives (see Philippians 2:13).

I may be a white-knuckled wreck when I consider the significance of my purpose, but I'm reminded that it's not really about me at all. No matter who or where we are, we have a lot to give, and we are "God's fellow workers" (1 Corinthians 3:9). What an honor! We are the hands of Jesus reaching out to others, making an eternal difference. Now that's what I call purpose!

Questions to STIR

1. Do you identify with Josie? How can you begin to see your life as more than your titles, roles and responsibilities?

2. How can you live more purposefully? If you are not sure of your purpose, pray and ask God to reveal His purpose for your life.

3. Read Romans 8:31. If God is "for you" how does this give you the courage to be "for" Him? How can you act on that courage?

Soul Sip Solutions

1. As a mom, how can you be the hands of Jesus to your family? What are little things you can do each day that will add up to a huge positive down the road? Make a list. Try to implement one thing this week.

2. Read 2 Timothy 1:9. God calls us to a "holy life" according to His "purpose." Journal what this means to you.

3. God can use us just as we are. Think of one way you can make a positive difference for God. Do it even if it scares you . . . especially if it scares you.

Reflections and Challenge

List things you are good at, like to do and that bring a sense of fulfillment to your life. Look for common themes. Ask God to further define your purpose and increase your effectiveness.

12

"EXTRA FOAM, PLEASE"

Wonder

Wonder is the basis of worship.
THOMAS CARLYLE

Let me understand the teaching of your precepts; then I will
meditate on your wonders.
PSALM 119:27

All I wanted to do was get a latte.

It was early November, and Starbucks was officially offering its gingerbread latte—a drink I'd waited for all year. Though it was rumored that certain baristas were serving it before the official release, I'd had no such luck. I'd driven to four different locations, finagling and begging for the holiday drink to no avail. Now, at last, I was just a toddler away, stuck outside the door.

My daughter Morgan was crouched close to the ground, transfixed, watching an army ant. An ant. The little black speck was moving a cookie crumb; and based on her level of interest, it was more exciting than the Disney Main Street parade.

"What's it doing, Mama? How's it carrying that cookie? Do ants like cookies? What kind of cookie is it? Where is it going?"

She fired off questions like the media at a presidential news conference. I answered as best . . . well, as fast as I could, but my mouth was dry with latte anticipation, my patience spent.

"She's probably taking the cookie back to her family for dinner," I said. "Hey, I have an idea . . . let's go inside. I'll buy you a cookie and we can sit on the patio and have our snack. We can drop a few crumbs and see if she comes back for more."

Jackpot.

Five minutes later, I was in gingerbread bliss, and Morgan had completely forgotten her little friend. She flittered about the patio collecting miniature acorns from a small scrub oak.

"Mommy, look!" she exclaimed, running over with a handful of squirrel nuts. "What are they?"

"Acorns," I replied, infinitely more patient now that I was in caffeine-sugar paradise.

"Can you eat them?"

"I think so," I said. "Native Americans used to grind them for food."

"Do they taste good?"

And the questions began again.

I sipped my drink and watched my little explorer investigate the patio, her natural curiosity bubbling up like a liter of root beer dropped on the floor.

"What does your drink taste like?" she asked, the mystery of the acorns satisfied.

"It's yummy, but not for kids. It's a mommy drink."

Her face fell . . . I softened.

"You can taste the bubbles if you want." I removed the lid, revealing cinnamon-sprinkled foam. I held it out for her, and like a frog after a fly, she flicked her tongue over the edge of the cup, catching a mouthful of bubbles in one lick. She kept her mouth open.

"Uh ubbles ah opping on i ung," she said, her tongue still sticking out as if she were catching snowflakes. She swallowed, then burst into giggles. "The bubbles were popping on my tongue!" she repeated.

The world's largest snowflake, found in 1887, was 15 inches wide and 8 inches thick. —Real Simple[1]

And so went our day, Morgan reopening my eyes to wonder. I often rush past discovery moments, not wanting to take the time to see beyond immediate need. My little monkey reminded me of the importance and delight in curiosity.

"Come on, George," I told her when it was time to go.

"Why are you calling me George?" she asked.

Beyond the Toy Box

According to Webster's dictionary, wonder is "to think or speculate curiously or to be filled with admiration, amazement, or awe."[2] My girls have more wonder than Linda Carter (*Wonder Woman*) and Fred Savage (*Wonder Years*) put together; they look upon the world with absorbent eyes, soaking in details like sponges, still believing in the impossible.

I have a lot to learn from them.

As a busy adult, I've put limits on what's possible. I have a university diploma hanging on my wall but have somehow forgotten that learning never ends—forgotten the world inside a flower, the magnificence of a dandelion carried on the wind and the joy in finding a lucky penny.

My daughters wear their princess dresses to the grocery store, identify cloud shapes in the sky and break the world sprint record when they hear the ice-cream man. For them, delight is everywhere. They are full of questions and observations: "Did God create that house? It's good He made a brick house, so the Big Bad Wolf can't blow it down!"

I smile at their sweet insights.

There is so much we adults don't see, our eyes blind with checklist cataracts. Peyton and Morgan want to dig up the backyard with spoons and catch bugs in my tea strainer . . . and it just may be the very same reason I want to try on a cute pair of heels at Nordstrom—*just to see*—because there is delight in discovery.

A sense of wonder is the cure-all for a ho-hum, melancholy existence. Wonder brings us a sense of appreciation and awe that allows us to see God in the ordinary: snow-capped mountains, a child's laughter, the intricate design of a robin's nest, a card in the mailbox when you need it most. God's hand is everywhere, painting the canvas of our lives. We just don't always see the strokes.

When You Least Expect It

Edward Young once said, "Wonder is involuntary praise." Embracing a sense of reverence and wonder for all that God has created is an act of praise; but all too often we take His blessings for granted. When I look at the world through my children's eyes, I pay attention, realizing a deeper appreciation for all, seeing and experiencing God in the details.

It helps to pay attention. Job 37:14 says to "stop and consider God's wonders." Psalm 9:1 says, "I will praise you, O Lord, with all of my heart; I will tell of all your wonders." As moms, we are blessed with little spiritual sages, helping us see the beautiful, the holy, the heavenly in every moment.

That is, if we let them.

Make a "wonder-full" date with your children:
Get blankets, snacks and a flashlight, then go stargazing
in the backyard before bed.

I don't know about you, but since I've become a mom, I've become preoccupied with safety. I like to know things are safe—that my children are protected and nourished. And while safety is good, my natural instinct is to be worried, hesitant and fearful for them. But the impetus behind risk-averse "safe" is fear, not faith. When things become too restricted and routine, we lose our sense of adventure and wonder. Playing it too safe kills the wind that would fill our sails and take us to the edge of the earth.

Fear squashes wonder like a bug under a shoe.

And just like that, wonder can vanish.

Children love to play Hide-and-Seek and Peekaboo. They love to be surprised by the "boogie man" in the closet and the "monster" behind the couch, and are ecstatic when they are. These games encourage discovery; our kiddos feel safe in exploring because they are confident in the protection of a nearby parent.

It is no different for us.

The unknown is scary.

We, too, need to feel safe in exploring, confident of God's protection.

A Cup of Wonder

Bringing wonder back into our lives takes faith in God's plan. God is the "heavenly Father" we can have confidence in. He is there with us in the Hide-and-Seek of life. Proverbs 14:26 says, "He who fears the LORD has a secure fortress, and for his children it will be a refuge."

Jesus did not play it safe. He said: Ask! Seek! Find! (See Luke 11:9-10.) Life is about discovery, learning, exploration . . . and wonder.

Consider the rhyme "Twinkle, Twinkle Little Star" that we hum to our little ones at night. Do we really wonder about the stars? How much of the "unknown" are we not seeing because we are not looking in faith?

Yes, we need "rules and reason" for our protection, but we were created to live in childlike faith and expectation (see Luke 18:16-17). More faith means more fun. Trust God. Step out—every day, every moment. Learn from your children. Explore with them. Look at the world from their point of view—with "kid eyes." But also be mindful of the ways in which our "Watch Out!" warnings can squelch their wonder-inspired spontaneity.

Delight in miracles. Believe in the impossible . . . for it can happen. A child's wonder is one of God's best miracles.

Our children are truly WONDER-full!

Questions to STIR

1. Do you embrace a sense of reverence and awe in your daily life? Are you too busy? Moving too fast? What can you learn from your child (children) in this area?

2. Do you have faith like a child, or tend to fear or doubt? Why/why not? Why do adults seem to lose their sense of wonder, wanting life to be so predictable that it's not fun anymore?

3. Look up 1 John 5:14. What does it mean to have confidence in God? How might this confidence change your approach to life?

Soul Sip Solutions

1. Consider the wonder in an average day. List the things that move you. Can you see God's design in the details?

2. Spend an afternoon outside with your children. No matter the weather, from sand to snow, let them investigate. Pay attention. Try to see every detail through their eyes.

3. Write a letter to God thanking Him for all the "wonder-full" things He has blessed you with.

Reflections and Challenge

From baking a cake with no lumps, to hearing your child sing, to having someone unload the dishwasher without being asked, list all the wonders and blessings you can think of in your life. Now put a star next to the ones God has a hand in. Do you see a pattern of God's presence?

I3

PERSONALIZED CONCOCTIONS

Inspiration and Creativity

We are not accustomed to thinking that God's will for us and our own inner dreams can coincide.
JULIA CAMERON, *THE ARTIST'S WAY*

In the beginning God created the heavens and the earth.
GENESIS 1:1

"I'm just not a creative person," said my friend Alex, as we stood in line at the local Starbucks.

"Yes, you are," I replied.

"Nope. I'm not at all. You—now *you* are creative, but I don't have a creative bone in my body. Some people are just wired that way and some of us are not."

"I don't believe that," I argued. "I think everyone has creative potential."

"No, no, no," Alex said emphatically, like a frustrated teacher. "I can't draw or paint. I can't even write very well and—"

"Excuse me," the barista interrupted. "What drink can I start for you ladies?"

"I'll have a Grande nonfat latte," I said.

"Hmmm," said Alex thoughtfully. "You know, I think I'll try something new today. I'll have a Venti mocha with half nonfat and half regular milk . . . and can you add raspberry syrup to that? And extra foam?"

"Sure," said the barista, writing frantically. "Do you want whipped cream?"

"Oh, yes! And some chocolate shavings—do you have those? And actually, can you add a pump of orange syrup too? I'd like to try that."

"Okay," said the barista. "So you want a Venti blended raspberry-orange mocha with extra foam, whip and chocolate shavings?"

"And extra hot," Alex added.

"Got it," said the barista, who, in my opinion, could have won an award for her attention to detail.

"So anyway," said Alex, turning back to me, "I'm just not creative at all."

Was she kidding?

My friend had the potential to be a drink designer for the Starbucks empire. She'd mixed flavors and tastes I never would have combined—just to try something new. Her inspiration was instant, with HDTV clarity. Still, she didn't see herself as "creative," because her gifts didn't fall into a preconceived art-box of drawing, painting or writing.

While we sipped our drinks, I teased Alex about her noncreative coffee. Meanwhile, she told me how she'd made an amazing soup the night before with "just the stuff I had in my kitchen."

Again I was incredulous. Alex was a chef, a designer, an artist in every sense, but failed to see her creative gifts; she was blind to her own talent.

Inspired Voice

We all have creative aptitude. All of us. God created the heavens and the earth and we are created in His image (see Genesis 1:27). This means, for any of you who haven't yet had your morning latte, that we all have creative potential—gazillions of it. My friend Alex didn't see it, but she had a very narrow perception of what constitutes creativity.

So what is creativity? It is the process of creating: inventing, making, developing. We get stuck when we associate creativity with art, music, poetry—things that seem to be "inspired" when in reality, creativity is, as my mom says, "a way of finding our way through the day." Creativity is arranging flowers for the dinner table, efficiently organizing our office or coordinating a romantic rendezvous with our spouse.

When I was growing up, my mom would make "Linda's Surprise" for dinner. What was it? We never really knew until we sat down to eat—and then perhaps still didn't know. "Linda's Surprise" was a mish-mash of whatever she had in the kitchen. As a kid, I thought it was a little bit weird, but it always tasted good. And there was always a bit of intrigue about what we'd have for dinner. Now, as a mom myself, I see her creative meals as brilliant solutions. I now make "Celeste's Surprise" all the time: I don't have to shop for special ingredients; I make do. It saves time, money, eliminates waste and gives my family an opportunity to try new things; dinner is never boring. I call this home-cooked creativity.

> "Invention, my dear friends, is 93 percent perspiration, 6 percent electricity, 4 percent evaporation, and 2 percent butterscotch ripple."
>
> —GENE WILDER, AS WILLY WONKA IN
> *CHARLIE AND THE CHOCOLATE FACTORY*[1]

Developing our creativity takes initiative. Thomas Edison said, "Genius is one percent inspiration and ninety-nine percent perspiration." Inspiration may be the idea behind the action, but taking initiative brings your idea into existence. Creativity is linked to perspiration, and much of the work is rooted in problem solving. Coloring in the scuffed heel of a boot with a black Sharpie is creative. Finding a way to make science fun for a room full of fifth-graders is creative. Finding a way to "clean" your house in 10 minutes is creative. Moms have countless opportunities to thoughtfully tackle problems with creative solutions, bringing their personal signature to ordinary obstacles, solving their daily dilemmas.

Plethora of Possibilities

Life offers us a plethora of possibilities to live out our dreams. What is your dream? Don't know? Get quiet. Listen. Do you know your dream but have no idea how to get there? Get creative. And get busy. Julia Cameron, in her book *The Artist's Way,* says, "We are not accustomed to thinking that God's will for us and our own inner dreams can coincide."[2] They can, but often we must be willing to prioritize, sacrifice, and sweat, cutting the superfluous time wasters from our schedule.

My friend Tandi is one of the most creative people I know. She does creative like cheesecake does tasty. She is a great painter (some of her work is sold at Target); she sings, plays guitar in a band, and home schools her two boys. Her house, clothes and even her hair have flair. Her boys are self-taught musicians and her youngest is a successful photographer. Her husband is equally creative, a very skilled graphic artist and computer whiz. Their secret? They work hard . . . and they don't own a television. Not one. Can you imagine having two teenage boys and no TV? She does. She and her husband have established a family culture that centers around discovering and developing their God-given talents, not being couch carrots. Imagine what your life would be if all your TV time was directed into developing your gifts and talents. What could you do?

Maybe you don't watch television, but you have a similar time waster. Mine was reading. Now don't put down your book just yet—hear me out. I love to read, but one day, frustrated that my writing career wasn't going anywhere, I said to my husband, "I wish I could sell an article." And he said, "You need to write more."

"I write a lot," I said.

"You read a lot," he said.

"Well, good writers need to read," I defended.

"Good writers need to write," he said. "You read more than you write."

His words resonated. Now, I am a book club flunky, but I am living my dream.

We all have different aptitudes and strengths, and there is so much in our creative-ability toolbox. Look for the opportunity. Create the time and allow God's fountain of inspiration to flow.

A Cup of Inspiration and Creativity

We can all make a positive difference by incorporating more creativity into our lives and taking steps toward our dreams. We have been created by an amazing, inspiring God, who knit us together in our mother's womb (see Psalm 139:13). He created the north and the south (see Psalm 89:12) and we are made in His likeness (see Genesis 5:1). With God setting the bar, we can at least step up and get crazy with dinner. We can look for problems to solve and ways to bless others with our gifts and talents. Creativity is not just artsty-fartsy stuff; it is concocting a great coffee, preparing a fabulous meal, putting the perfect accessory with an outfit. It is painting fingernails at a retirement home and sharing your story. It is putting a blueberry smiley face on your child's pancake. It is making the effort.

Marcelle Shriver is an example of proactive creativity. This mother of an American soldier serving in Iraq heard that Silly String sprayed in doorways helps detect bomb tripwires. So she started a campaign to collect cans of the party goo for the troops, spearheading the collection drive, using her energy and talents to help save lives.[3]

I think God wants us all to tap our creative potential. I believe we are called to give the world the best we have. How can we do that? If you, like a hungry guest at a Thanksgiving dinner, don't know where to start, then get creative about your quiet time. As Etty Hillesum once said, "I do believe it is possible to create, even without ever writing a word or painting a picture, but simply by molding one's inner life. And that too is a deed." Look to God for creative inspiration. Pray. Go for a walk. Look at all He has created. Worship.

"Life is not easy for any of us. But what of that? We must have perseverance and above all confidence in ourselves. We must believe we are gifted for something . . ." —Marie Curie[4]

Isaiah 43:7 says that we are created for God's glory. He surrounds us in glorious, creative blessings: the twinkling eyes of our children, a field of wildflowers, birds whistling a sonnet, spontaneous laughter. We bring glory to God with our lives when we use our talents. Sing to Him, forgive a wrong, unload the dishwasher without whining, go on a scavenger hunt with your kids, romance your husband. Taking thoughtful action to love others is creativity at its best, and it honors God, too. So, get to it.

Questions to STIR

1. Consider the fact that God is creativity. Since you are created in His image, you are a creative being. How do you embrace your creative side? How might you further develop these talents and gifts?

2. Eric Hoffer said, "Man is most uniquely human when he turns obstacles into opportunities." What is holding you back from your dreams? How can you creatively turn your obstacles into opportunities?

3. Read Psalm 139:13; Isaiah 44:2; Isaiah 49:5 and Psalm 22:9. Ponder the verses. You were "knit together" by God. What does that mean to you, and how does it affirm your worth and value?

Soul Sip Solutions

1. When you think of creativity, what comes to mind? Brainstorm ways that you are or have been creative in the last week. Can't think of any? Think again.

2. What are your untapped creative aspirations? If it is to learn to draw, take a class. If it is learning to cook, make a recipe with a friend. Think of one way to take creative action toward a more inspired life, and do it.

3. Go for a walk and observe all that God has created.

Reflection and Challenge

List 10 ways you can take thoughtful action to creatively love those who are most important to you. Pray and ask God to help you bring these creative ideas to fruition.

_____

_____

_____

_____

_____

_____

_____

_____

_____

_____

_____

_____

_____

_____

_____

_____

_____

_____

_____

_____

_____

_____

_____

COFFEE BREAK
WITH TANDI

Dear Moms,

As I witness storm clouds majestically form bright-white towering giants against a deep indigo sky, I am left breathless. You've seen the diving dolphin with an elephant trunk riding the one-winged dragon chasing the sheep skating across the sky, right? Aah-h-h . . . cloud gazing, one of my favorite pastimes.

I'm a wonderer. It's my "time-in" with God. I watch Him paint passionately with light, color, vapor, wind. I gasp in amazement at His grandeur—a love song's caressing melody where the lover never ceases singing. It's an epic love story that goes on and on.

Are you aware of God's timeless, unceasing love? Have you taken time to look at the exquisite masterpieces He makes for *you*, every day? Just look at every detail: sights, sounds, sensations, smiles.

For me, creativity, wonder and gratitude are inseparable. My eagerness to create, whether knitting a scarf or inventing a delectable dish for dinner, begins with a burning sensation, an irrepressible must-do, which springs from times with God. His wonder-filled creation and the intricacy of the world around inspire me.

An environment for wondering is evident in our home: Paint tubes and canvases are ready for the next Picasso. Musical instruments are resident in almost every room. (Yes, even the kind I sometimes regret having, when the neighbor rings the doorbell, not to invite us to the barbecue, but . . .)

I am often asked questions like "Mom, can I get an old motorcycle to take apart *and* put it back together again?" These activities, while filling the garage with motorcycle parts and grease, keep the engine of creativity, initiative and determination running in two teenagers.

Grateful that we went years without the distractions of time wasters, I'm pleased to say that my kids continue to create. Yes, they're made in His image, too . . . though sometimes I wonder.

Tandi Venter

AN ESSENTIAL INGREDIENT

Respect

❖

*He who does not have the courage to speak up for his rights
cannot earn the respect of others.*
RENE G. TORRES

Show proper respect to everyone.
1 PETER 2:17

"I am completely underwater," Melissa confided as we huddled in
the corner of the coffee shop, her eyes tired, as though she had not
slept since I'd last seen her. "I can't take on one more responsibility or I'll be headed for divorce court. I'm so busy, sometimes I can't
even find time to shower." She tipped the lid of her baseball cap in
my direction and rolled her eyes, "Like today."

 *According to information cited in "Have You Gone
Caffeine Crazy?" in the* Ladies' Home Journal, *too much
caffeine can magnify the effects of stress.* [1]

"You need to clear your plate," I told her. "You don't have to do
everything."

"I know, I just don't know what to cut. I am so involved in organizing the fall fundraiser at Lucy's school, I'd feel bad to back
out now."

"Well, what else can go?" I asked.

"I'm not sure anything can. I'm serving in two ministries at church and they are short on volunteers—*they need me*; plus, just driving the kids around to all their activities is hectic, but I can't ask them to stop doing sports."

It was apparent that Melissa, who was extremely capable and talented, had become the "go to" person for way too much—volunteering at school and church, running a home-based business and keeping her household afloat while her husband traveled several days a week for his job. She had taken on responsibilities slowly, over time, but like a frog in a soup pot, she hadn't noticed the water heating up until it was boiling.

"Maybe you need to learn to say no and not feel bad about it," I suggested, in teacher mode.

"I know."

Our conversation trailed on to other things: our children, recipes, reality TV. Then the bell on the café door jingled us to attention.

A raven-haired woman in a brick-red turtleneck and dark jeans made her way to the coffee counter—then turned and spotted us.

"Melissa!" she called across the room. "I can't believe you're here! I've been meaning to call you."

Like a guard dog, I sat at attention. My eyes darted to Mel.

"How are you, Irene?" asked Melissa, with a sagging smile. The woman grabbed her coffee and walked over.

"I'm good, same old stuff," she replied. "Hey, I'm coordinating the teacher luncheon next Wednesday and wondered if you would make your famous enchiladas?"

"Oh, I dunno, I'm so busy right now. I'm not sure I can."

"What a bummer," said Irene. "Everyone loved them when you made them last year. They'll be so disappointed. Can't you make a teensy exception?"

"Well, maybe I could make a quick batch," she relented. "When do you need them?"

Recognizing Boundaries: Yours and Others

Sometimes it's hard to say no. I often find myself in Melissa's situation—overwhelmed and barely able to keep my head above water.

Then I'll be asked to do something and cave, adding another rock of responsibility to my mountain. I understand why Melissa gave in; she didn't want to let everyone down and admitted later that she was flattered that her enchiladas were in high demand. In the moment, any request is apt to feel small; but like sun exposure, it is the cumulative effect that does the damage.

In saying she'd bring the Mexican dish, she committed herself to shop for ingredients, set aside time to bake and deliver them. That was two hours she didn't have.

"I'll just make a double recipe and save some for dinner," she said with a shrug.

There are always ways to justify something you shouldn't have signed up for in the first place, and a lot of wonderful causes and organizations to support that legitimately need volunteers. Opportunities are endless. That still doesn't mean we should overcommit: No matter what we do, there will always be a need.

Now let me clarify: Service is very important. Sharing our gifts and talents is a huge blessing to others and can be very rewarding. The problem arises when we get so overextended that we suffer—our families, ourselves. If we are so busy "serving" that we can't find time to shower, that's a problem. If we are so involved "doing" for others that our family life feels harried (or nonexistent), then we need to evaluate our priorities. What's truly most important?

It all comes down to respect.

When I was younger, I remember struggling with peer pressure. I wanted to do what the other kids were doing; I wanted to be liked, not left out. I talked with my parents about it and my dad said, "It is better to be respected than liked. Anyone can give in to pressure. It takes a strong person to stand up for what is right." His words stuck with me, and now, as a mom, the same principle applies: I strive for balance by setting and maintaining boundaries based on what is best for me and my family. That's respect.

Honoring God by Honoring Yourself

It is important for each of us to recognize that saying no does not constitute a lack of value for the sponsoring person or organization. For example, how many times have you been invited to a home party where items are sold? Do you feel obligated to go and purchase something? I have. For years, I attended these parties, not so much for the merchandise, but to keep in touch with friends. Eventually, needing to tighten finances, I stopped attending and discovered something amazing: I didn't miss these outings. Even though I occasionally saw a friend or two, rarely did I truly connect with them. I often left feeling tired, broke and sometimes even irritated at the time wasted.

"The truth is, saying no can be hard. It involves putting our own desires and needs above the wishes and expectations of others, which clashes with our natural inclination to be generous."

—Nanette Gartrell, M.D., Ladies' Home Journal[2]

Saying no is difficult—especially when you may miss what seems like a fun outing. Still, time and energy are better spent on activities that refresh and add to our lives rather than detract. (Ahem. Easier said than done.) After years of going along with the crowd, I am *starting* to learn that health—and children who remember my name—is much more important than popularity. I am becoming ruthless about eliminating energy drains—and just as important, learning to say yes to things that fill up my cup. Connecting with Jesus in quiet time affirms, refreshes and gives me hope; Bible study also contributes to spiritual growth and a true sense of purpose— a much better use of my time.

Remember: You can say no to most anything that drains you. Saying no to a church-related activity is not necessarily saying no to God; in fact, creating a balance with family and other commitments honors Him. We are not called to be stretched like Cling Wrap, but to be good stewards of our time, talents and gifts. Respect yourself! Say no to the activities that drain—and yes to those that sustain.

Not long ago, a friend asked me to help edit a book she was writing. Though I wanted to help her, I knew I couldn't give the project my time and attention.

"I'm sorry, I'd love to, but I just can't," I told her.

"I'll pay you," she continued.

"No, it's not the money. I just know that if I tried to do that and my own stuff right now, neither would get my full attention. That's not fair to you or me."

"Really? Even a little help would be great," she pleaded.

"I just can't," I told her.

And then, though she might have felt disappointed, she smiled and said, "Hmm. Good boundaries."

Benjamin Franklin once said, "The best thing to give to your enemy is forgiveness; to an opponent, tolerance; to a friend, your heart; to your child, a good example; to a father, deference; to your mother, conduct that will make her proud of you; to yourself, respect; to all men, charity." I like this quote. It reminds me that I can't give my best to anything if I do not respect myself—and honor my own needs first. If I overcommit to activities, I can't give my heart to my friends, much less find the time to call them. I can't give my children a good example if I'm never home or constantly on my computer. A good example is a well-rounded, balanced life—one that models service, yes, but also healthy, growing relationships, passion and fun.

If we are not used to saying no, it can take a while to build our doormat spines into sturdy backbones. We must know our core values and determine our priorities around what honors them. Press through feelings of guilt for not committing and even for backing out of something. (Backing out might provide an opportunity for someone else.) Be okay with saying no, even if it will disappoint. Respecting ourselves is honoring our needs in the little and big decisions of everyday life—allowing us to enjoy what really matters, instead of half-heartedly schlepping through obligations we don't really care about, that add little value to our lives.

A Cup of Respect

The Bible talks a lot about respect. In 1 Thessalonians 4:12, we are told to live in such a way that our daily lives will win respect. We are to show proper respect to everyone (see 1 Peter 2:17) and honor others. We are told to respect our mother and father (see Leviticus 19:3), show respect to the elderly (see Leviticus 19:32), and respect our husbands (see Ephesians 5:33). It starts with family, communicating respect through ordinary details and actions. It is maintaining good boundaries, balance and clear priorities.

It feels good to get rave reviews on a plate of tasty enchiladas or anything we make or do. However, when we look to others for validation and kudos, we are looking in the wrong place; our worth, our value comes from God.

Often doing what we can to help others means going above and beyond the duties of the average day; however, if we don't work from a place of respecting our own needs first, then we will ultimately fail—so busy and overcommitted that we are rendered useless. If we are fabulous volunteers at the expense of our health, marriage or relationships, what's the point? What really matters?

Respecting yourself means looking to God for your value and setting healthy boundaries in all areas of life. Seek God's guidance and direction. It's not always easy, but when we live from this place, we will not only respect ourselves and others, but we will also experience fulfillment, blessing and grace—and that's the whole enchilada.

Questions to STIR

1. Do you identify with Melissa? Do you have a hard time saying no to requests and take on more responsibility than you can handle? If so, why? What is the core need/motivation driving your action?

2. Do you set a positive example for your children, respecting yourself—your body and needs? In what ways might you be a better role model?

3. First Peter 2:17 says to show proper respect to everyone. Is there someone in your life to whom you are not showing proper respect? How can you change your behavior and make amends?

Soul Sip Solutions

1. Think about all your commitments and activities. Do you have too much on your plate? If so, what are the biggest stressors? Brainstorm three ways to phase out of some of your responsibilities or find someone to replace you in these areas.

2. Don't do anything. Just sit and rest for five minutes. Close your eyes, breathe deeply, and appreciate the moment.

3. Practice saying no gracefully. The next time you are asked to do something, if you cannot do it, decline without guilt. If you can do it, accept with enthusiasm. (But say no first, just for practice.)

Reflection and Challenge

Respecting yourself and others takes an awareness of (1) values, (2) priorities and (3) boundaries. What matters to you most? From your relationship with God, to your family, career and so on, list the things you cherish. Are you spending your time and attention proportionately in these areas? If not, how can you adjust?

_____

_____

_____

_____

_____

_____

_____

_____

_____

_____

_____

15

COFFEE AND DONUTS

Health and Wellness

A balanced diet is a cookie in each hand.
AUTHOR UNKNOWN

Do you not know that your body is a temple of the Holy Spirit, who is in you, whom you have received from God? You are not your own.
1 CORINTHIANS 6:19

"You can't just rely on caffeine for energy," says my sister, a personal life coach. "I bet if you exercise on a regular basis, you'll feel way better."

"Yeah, I'm sure exercise will help. Thanks for the advice," I say as I hang up the phone.

Exercise . . . what's THAT? I wondered. "Exercise" was a word that had once existed in my vocabulary, but since becoming a mom, I couldn't quite remember exactly what it was. A busy schedule, fatigue and brain cell loss from two pregnancies had obviously done nothing for my retention skills.

Then it slowly began to come back to me: "Exorcize" . . . moving on a Stairmaster for an extended period to cast off any demons causing me to gobble forbidden amounts of Sour Patch Kids. No. That didn't seem quite right.

I listed all the "Ex" words I could think of to trigger my memory: *Exert. Exorbitant. Excrete. Execrable. Exhaustion. Excuse. Excursion. Exempt.* As I rattled off the words, my synapses started to snap: *Oh, now I remember:* Exercise is *exerting* an *exorbitant* amount of energy until my body begins to *excrete* sweat. It is an *execrable* activity, usually resulting in *exhaustion.* High school physical education classes were centered around exercise. I recall always wanting to have an *excuse* to go on an *excursion* so that I could be *exempt* from P.E.

It was just like my sister to extol the benefits of such an energy intensive endeavor. Exercise was work. Sure, it would make me feel better—after exercising, the rest of my day would seem like a vacation: I could change a messy diaper in 30 seconds, make a PBJ sandwich in 2 minutes, fold a basket of laundry in 5, bathe the kids in 15, and make dinner in 25. But, exercise? If memory served me correctly, it required at least 30 minutes of continuous effort. No thank you, Sis.

Chewing Is *Not* Exercise

I don't know about you, but for me, sticking to a regular exercise program is about as easy as getting tickets to Oprah: it doesn't happen often. I always have the best of intentions—and I know all the benefits, but when push comes to shove, I shove the exercise.

"Thirty million Americans drink specialty coffee beverages daily." —E-Imports[1]

Doesn't everything seem more urgent than the treadmill? Isn't the lemon-frosted pound cake at Starbucks just the perfect accompaniment to a latte? Most of the time where there is an intention to exercise, there is an urgent *something* that has sabotaged my workout—oatmeal for breakfast and a spinach salad for lunch become a caffeinated drink and a sugary snack in my paw, sustaining me like an addict until late afternoon when my blood sugar tanks, leaving me cranky and exhausted.

I've got to get my act together. Not only do I want to be around to be a grandmother, I want to have a good quality of life. I don't mind aging, but I don't want to look like my face has been forgotten in the washing machine—all wrinkly, creased and sour. We moms sacrifice our needs, coasting on the myth that we'll take care of ourselves later, but later never comes, and time takes its toll:

A dental check-up after the birth of my second child revealed I had SIX cavities. The muscle tone in my legs went on vacation and never returned. Cellulite is trying to stake a claim on the back of my triceps. Osteoporosis threatens from lack of exercise and too much caffeine. Wearing jeans that are too tight gives me a "muffin top."

This laundry list of neglect is easy to overlook or push aside. Except for when I get anxious. When I lack a physical outlet for my stress, I become uneasy, irritable and short-tempered. At these times, I am not even close to the mom God has created me to be.

A Better Way

Maintaining overall wellness is a huge part of giving our best to others. Physical, mental and spiritual health—all are integral components in functioning our best. Neglect in one area affects the others.

There are many components to good physical health, but the two biggies are proper nutrition and regular exercise. Now, you know your own liabilities, but if you skip breakfast or subsist on a latte 'til noon, it may be time to revamp your diet. Think baby steps. If you are a breakfast skipper, just having a bowl of Cheerios with your kids in the morning can help get you into the habit of eating a morning meal. Then after a while, you can transition to an egg-white and asparagus omelet—okay, well, a bowl of oatmeal. (Try this tasty recipe: One serving old-fashioned oatmeal with $1/2$ cup blueberries, 1 tablespoon ground flaxseed, several dashes of cinnamon, a bit of brown sugar, and $1/2$ cup skim milk. Stir it all up and enjoy. It is so yum and gives me tons of energy!)

Look for little ways to establish good practices and work the healthy stuff into your diet. If you've found crafty ways to get broccoli into your toddler's diet, then you should be able to get more green stuff onto your own plate.

I know exercise is important, and when I work out, I see an immediate improvement not only in my attitude but also in my desire to take better care of myself overall. The stress-relief component cannot be overestimated—physical release through exercise peels me like an artichoke, removing the prickly bits of tension, stress and anxiety, leaving my heart tender and ready to love.

I find it works best to get up early before my kids or incorporate exercise into activities I can do with them. Walking to the park together, riding bikes, swimming, skiing, baking cookies—it all counts as exercise. Well, baking counts, but only if you jump rope with your children while each batch is in the oven.

Walking to the park together, riding bikes, swimming, skiing, baking cookies—it all counts as exercise. Well, baking counts, but only if you jump rope with your kids while each batch is in the oven.

Mental health is also key. Having a good self-concept, participating in activities you value and feel are important and having a creative outlet are all components of metal health. An appropriate outlet for anger and frustration (think kick-boxing or running) is good too. I feel the best when I am taking care of myself physically and am grounded on a spiritual level.

A Cup of Spiritual Health

True health and wellness happen when we have a balanced diet of fruits and vegetables—*and* a balanced diet of God's Word; when we have regular workouts and regularly exercise our faith. Spiritual health happens when we look to God for our strength and then s-t-r-e-t-c-h into who and what He has called us to be. Ephesians 6:10 says to "be strong in the Lord and in his mighty power." When God is our strength, we can overcome. We can choose wisely and we can honor Him by honoring ourselves, not running ourselves into the ground thinking we'll make health and wellness a priority later. This mentality robs us of good health.

First Corinthians 6:19 reminds us that our bodies are temples of the Holy Spirit. Sometimes I forget this, trying to maintain my temple on a mocha and a double chocolate brownie. It doesn't work. We have the strength that raised Jesus from the dead, but seriously, how do we tap into it when we can't even get out of bed in the morning? Good question. Again: Baby steps.

Ask God to help you.

Carve out a few minutes of quiet time in the morning.

Read your Bible and pray.

Load your iPod with a devotional and listen while you are on the elliptical trainer.

Sing worship songs with your kids in the car.

The more you reach out to Jesus, the stronger your spiritual muscles will get. Flex them and honor Him.

First Chronicles 16:11 says, "Look to the LORD and his strength; seek his face always." When I do this, it's a heck of a lot easier to make good decisions and stay positive. My life flows better. I am filled with peace. I am a better mom. I choose broccoli and take the stairs.

There will always be things that compete with what's most important. Be diligent and passionate, creatively seeking ways to make health and wellness a priority: physical health, mental health and spiritual health. God is watching out for us. He sends us little reminders all the time. Just the other day I was reading Proverbs 4:23, which said, "Above all else, guard your heart, for it is the wellspring of life" and I thought, *I need to be careful about gossip and idle chat . . . and I really need to get some cardiovascular exercise and take my fish oil!*

I doubt the latter is anywhere close to the theological application of that verse, but you know what? It spoke to me . . . and I hit the treadmill.

Questions to STIR

1. Do you tend to make health and wellness a priority, or do you push your needs to the back burner?

2. How do you think spiritual, mental and physical health are related? Can you have one strong area without the other?

3. Do you treat your body as a temple of the Holy Spirit or as a dumping ground for caffeine, sugar and leftovers? How does the reminder that God dwells within us change your perspective of how you treat your body?

Soul Sip Solutions

1. If you have been lacking either physical or spiritual exercise, make it a priority to get at least two "workouts" in this week.

2. Think of creative ways to exercise with your kids, incorporating physical and spiritual exercise. Ideas include: Go for a walk, sing songs to God, ride your bikes, have a short Bible study together.

3. Make a tasty, healthy meal for your family. Take the time to thank God for the nourishment He provides.

Reflection and Challenge

Is it harder for you to stay "fit" in physical exercise or spiritual discipline? Brainstorm a few ways to incorporate more "exercises" into your daily life and routine.

_____

_____

_____

_____

_____

_____

_____

_____

_____

_____

_____

_____

_____

_____

16

KEEPING IT FRESH

Courtship and Marriage

A successful marriage requires falling in love many times,
always with the same person.
MIGNON MCLAUGHLIN

Be kind and compassionate to one another, forgiving each other,
just as in Christ God forgave you.
EPHESIANS 4:32

"I'm just going to stop at the store and then I'll be home."

"Okay, sounds good," said Anthony. "I'm on my way home, too, so I'll see you in a bit." As he hung up his cell, Anthony saw Coleen's SUV turn across the intersection, toward the grocery store.

I think I'll get the kids so that she doesn't have to manage them at the store, he thought, following Coleen into the parking lot.

But as Coleen drove through the lot, she thought, *There is no way I can handle the kids at the store right now . . . I am so tired. I'm going to go get a coffee.* She circled, turned back onto the street and headed to Starbucks.

Where the heck is she going? Anthony wondered, now following his wife like a police cruiser in pursuit. When Coleen pulled into the drive-thru, Anthony pulled in behind her. He tried to get her attention in the rearview mirror, waving and smiling, but she wasn't paying attention. He tried calling, but she wasn't answering her cell; she was likely on the phone with someone else, ignoring his call, oblivious to the fact that he was right behind her in the coffee queue.

Anthony waited. He waved. Coleen did not notice him.

Then he had an idea.

He backed out of line, parked and walked in. He went up to the counter, asked for the manager and introduced himself.

"My wife is in the drive-thru, but she doesn't know I'm here," he explained. "Is there any way I can serve her coffee to her?" he asked.

"Sure," replied the manager, handing him a green apron and taking him back to the drive-thru window.

As Coleen approached, she was, as Anthony suspected, engrossed in conversation on her cell. She handed her cash through the window without looking at the attendant. Then Anthony stepped in.

"Here is your Grande Caramel Macchiato," he said, passing the coffee into her outstretched hand.

"Thanks," she said, still not making eye contact.

"I have to tell you, you are the most beautiful woman I've ever seen," Anthony said, keeping hold of her hand.

At this, she jolted, looked at him and screamed.

"Oh my gosh, Anthony! What are you doing here?"

The kids in the backseat craned their necks to see what was happening. Upon seeing his dad in the window, young Michael said, "Hey, Daddy works at Starbucks!"

The Toll of Time

What a fun story! I love Anthony's spontaneity and effort toward his marriage. Marriage takes work—in the big and little details—to keep love strong and maintain commitment over the long haul. Yet in today's society, we've become accustomed to drive-thru ease. We want it all; we update, upgrade, order in, take out, shop online, rarely denying ourselves. But the convenience mentality doesn't serve us well in marriage. We all want the best from our marriages—and our expectations are high—so when things don't go as planned, it's imperative that we stay the course through the bumps and curves.

When things go awry in a marriage, it is easy to focus on what's lacking. Whether it's good communication, financial stability, sexual intimacy, laughter or whatever, the grass can look greener elsewhere. But the truth is: "The grass is greener where you water it!"

My pastor, Greg Thompson, said this one Sunday morning, and the message touched my heart. I needed to "water" my marriage through loving action and prayer.

"With patience and tenderness she gradually brought the light of understanding to his darkened, obtuse mind and he discovered the joy of loving someone, with all his heart."

—RONALD REAGAN, PRESIDENT OF THE UNITED STATES, IN A LETTER
TO HIS WIFE NANCY, MARCH 4, 1981[1]

I love Coleen's story. She can recall numerous love-capades like that. "My husband is so thoughtful. The little things he does mean so much."

It's not that they have a perfect union; they, like all of us, have issues and troubles. However, they have discovered the art of keeping their marriage fresh and fun through intentional, loving action.

No matter how compatible a couple may seem, life can set them adrift like pieces of a glacier, floating farther away from each other in an icy cold sea of accumulated hurts and disappointments; their hearts can slowly harden like Play-Doh in a cracked container. (If you've accumulated much of the hardened Play-Doh, you may want to consider professional Christian "couples" counseling to help you in reconciliation and renewal of your marriage commitment.)

You may have heard the expression from Francis Edward Smedley: "All's fair in love and war." While that may imply that all sorts of tactics are "fair" in order to win (your way), I'm not so sure it makes for a successful marriage. As clever as it may seem, and as much as we try to convince ourselves it's for the good, manipulation and other dishonest tactics never result in a more loving, healthy relationship. Take responsibility for your relationship and turn your intention toward building your marriage with solid-gold bricks of love.

Gold Bricks of Love

So what are some of these gold bricks you can use to keep your marriage fresh and strong? Consider the following:

- *Pray for your marriage.* List areas in your marriage that need attention and pray about them on a daily basis. Be specific—and know that God answers your prayers. Stormie Omartian, in *The Power of a Praying Wife*, says, "The power that resurrected Jesus is the very same power that will resurrect the dead places of your marriage and put life back into it."[2] If your relationship has stalemated, ask God to reveal if the holdup is in your heart. Pray every day, with every action, and at every opportunity. And have people who know and love both of you pray for your marriage too.

- *Spend time together and make communication a priority.* Plan date nights and weekend getaways. Make these times ironclad; schedule them as recurring meetings in your PDA (and your mind). Look for opportunities to make every moment special: Get up early and have coffee-chat together before the day starts; cook dinner together; take a bath together and catch up after your children go to bed. Get creative and take action.

- *Forgive and trust.* Be honest about your feelings and needs, then release your husband to the Lord, trusting that God is big enough to deal with his stuff—and yours.

- *Be humble.* Don't keep score; marriage is not a game. Look for ways to make your partnership better, and do them, even if it feels like you are the only one making the effort. Loving is a choice; choose to love your partner even when you don't feel like it. Think *accept*—not *expect*. Don't qualify what you're willing to give by what you expect in return. Believe me, you will both be happier.

- *Be thoughtful and encouraging, open and honest.* Be each other's biggest fan. Share your needs. Speak the truth, but bite your tongue when what you plan to say is neither kind nor helpful. The underlying message of careless words can cause irreparable damage.

- *See your spouse through God's eyes.* When you see each other from God's point of view, it will give you an "extreme makeover" of the heart, revealing attractive qualities in abundance.

Love is in the details, and when it comes to marriage, many small efforts over a lifetime pay big dividends. Remember: You are both on the same team.

A Cup of Courtship

We all know the statistics; divorce is commonplace and almost expected in our culture. It's a tough world; daily stresses pull a marriage apart like cotton candy in a tug-of-war. And as such, maintaining a strong bond can be hard to do in our own strength.

We need God's strength.

God loves us with perfect love. If we look to Him to fill our cup— to cover our needs—that abundance will overflow onto our spouse. Our spouse can never meet all of our needs (*and he isn't supposed to!*).

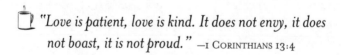 *"Love is patient, love is kind. It does not envy, it does not boast, it is not proud."* —I Corinthians 13:4

First Corinthians 13:4-8 reminds us, "Love is patient, love is kind. It does not envy, it does not boast, it is not proud. It is not rude, it is not self-seeking, it is not easily angered, it keeps no record of wrongs. Love does not delight in evil but rejoices with the truth. It always protects, always trusts, always hopes, always perseveres." This passage is often read at weddings, and it's good to reread it often and remind ourselves of these truths.

Life may pit us against each other, but it doesn't have to be that way. God has a different and winning game plan for us—one that definitely includes a daily, fresh-brewed cup of courtship, romance and lasting love.

Questions to STIR

1. Think of an argument or a disagreement you've had with your spouse that didn't come to an ideal resolution. What emotions affected your comments or behavior? How could you have reacted differently for the sake of your marriage?

2. Read 1 Corinthians 13. Love is an action. Based on this passage, how can you show more love to your spouse? Do you always protect, hope and persevere? What limits your love?

3. Think of what a gift it would be to your children to have a mom and dad who cherish each other; how might you better love your children by making an effort toward your spouse?

Soul Sip Solutions

1. Write a love letter to your husband. List all of the ways you love him. Tell him that "he's da man." Then tuck the letter in his suitcase when he travels for work or tape it to his side of the mirror in the bathroom.

2. Think of three practical ways you can show love to your husband (wash his car and fill the tank with gas, make him chips and dip while he watches his favorite team, take out the trash, and so on) and do it. Resist the urge to point out your effort.

3. Think of a time when you felt hurt by your husband. Pray and surrender this issue to God, even if your husband has not apologized. Keep giving it to God until the chains of the pain are

broken and you can extend true forgiveness to your partner. For the good of your marriage, let God work in your heart— and your husband's.

Reflection and Challenge

Write down some plans for a romantic date with your husband. Pick something (a restaurant or activity) that he would enjoy, even if it is out of your comfort zone, and do it. Make the extra effort.

_____

_____

_____

_____

_____

_____

_____

_____

_____

_____

_____

_____

_____

_____

_____

_____

_____

_____

_____

COFFEE BREAK
WITH LINDA

Dear Moms,

When people discover that my husband and I have been married 40 years, many ask, "What's your secret?" (Maybe both of us are good judges of character. Or perhaps it's that we start each day with him bringing me coffee.)

Giving the question some thought, I offer these secrets:

First, *trust God to love you*. After the honeymoon, you will discover who you've really married. Don't get caught up longing for an "ideal" partner. People grow and change. My husband and I are not the same people we were 40 years ago. We don't even look the same. When our daughters first saw our wedding photo, they asked, "Who are those people?" Be confident in God's love and you will learn love and acceptance for each other.

Second, *communicate honestly*. This takes personal integrity. Give your husband the opportunity to love the real you.

Third, *learn to negotiate*. As a businessman, my husband negotiates every day; me, not so much. As a nurse, I followed "doctor's orders." But I've learned that all of life is a negotiation. Here's a simple example from our now seasoned marriage: Recently, I mentioned wanting candles to put by the bathtub.

"Where are the candles I bought?" asked my husband. "You mean the ones that look like mugs full of beer?" I ask suspiciously. "They're in the pantry. Why?" "You wanted candles," he answers. "You could use those." (I know he's trying to be generous—and economical: Why buy more?) So I give him the courtesy of considering his offer, and then I say, "I have something different in mind."

There was a time when I would have felt it necessary to agree with his economics and concede. Then I would have "brewed" about it. So be assertive, fair and tactful. Express your preferences and learn to negotiate for them. It will help you with your husband . . . your teenager, and your two-year-old.

Blessings,
Linda Titcomb

17

WILL THAT BE A SMALL OR A TALL?

Financial Savvy

Do not value money for any more nor any less than its worth;
it is a good servant but a bad master.
ALEXANDRE DUMAS

No one can serve two masters. . . . You cannot serve both God and Money.
MATTHEW 6:24

By my calculations, I should be driving a Ferrari. Four dollars a day for 15 years is $21,900 spent for coffee. Okay, so maybe it won't buy a sports car, but I could have paid off a minivan by now if not for my coffee habit. It gets worse. Marketers have targeted the leg-clinging toddler standing in line with me. In the time it takes me to order up a gingerbread latte, little Morgan has grabbed a chocolate milk, a fruit cup and a stuffed toy from the thigh-level display to add to my tab. Talk about a "latte factor." I may not have a Ferrari (who cares, no room for car seats), but my kids just helped me drink my Jimmy Choos.

Resourcefulness Rules

The coffee habit, like a two-by-four, is hard to break. I love my morning coffee, especially when I have the opportunity to pick up a drink at a café; but I don't really need to buy the custom caffeination— I just want it. My friend Sue says she fights with herself, wondering, *Do I really need it? No. But I want it.* She tells me, "If I have the cash in my wallet, I usually buy it, then wonder if I'm wasting my money."

I've wondered the same thing; so when my sister-in-law went on a 40-day spending fast, I decided to try it too. Though at one time I was quite frugal with my finances, as my income increased, so did my propensity for spending. In fact, I'd developed some bad habits—such as a "replace it" mentality and an inability to walk into Target without spending at least a hundred bucks. To be honest, I wasn't sure of my true habits—other than my latte routine, which I knew was significant.

Two weeks into my spending fast, I was ransacking my office, looking for a coffee gift card. I rationalized that a prepaid card wasn't really "spending." When I found the card, however, it only had $5 on it, forcing me to go with home brew for the duration.

According to LivingWithBadCredit.com, "67 percent of people who signed up for a store credit card last holiday season say they were still paying off the bill eight months later." —SELF MAGAZINE[1]

Though I saved a lot of cash during my spending hiatus, ultimately what I gained most—and unexpectedly—was a deeper appreciation for what I already owned. I learned to be resourceful; when I normally would have just shelled out cash without thinking, I investigated and found no-cost options to fill my needs. I checked out books at the library that I normally would have purchased; I plucked my eyebrows instead of having them waxed; I wrote "100 Reasons Why I Love You" in journals (that I unearthed in my office) for birthday gifts; I had a potluck party and invited everyone via Evite, saving the cost of food, paper invitations and stamps; I used frequent flyer miles to book a trip.

I discovered that I needed to be a much better steward of my money and resources. Less really is more—and the more I simplified, the easier things became. I realized I'd become a thoughtless spender, justifying my purchases in the moment, but not really counting the true cost—to my pocketbook, debt ratio, closet capacity and the environment. Now don't misunderstand: I still shop at Target and go to Starbucks on occasion, but my careless spending days (and three-times-a-week latte routine) are history.[2]

Successful Simplicity

As moms, there are things we can do to better manage our financial resources. First, make a budget and then stick to it. (Budgets are great on paper, but like a reused Post-It note, it's hard to get them to stick.) Consider big financial decisions together with your spouse, and don't buy any significant purchase on impulse. Pray. Get some distance from that shiny black Jeep, red gas stove or the item you saw on eBay and make sure the purchase grooves with your financial means and long-term values.

Meet friends at the park or at the gym, not at the mall where all the cute new styles and clothes make it easy to *jones* for new junk. When you must go to the mall, shop with a list. Know what you need, and don't stray. If you see something you love, again, wait before you buy. Spend a couple days thinking about the item to make sure you can't live without it—or better yet, wait for it to go on sale. (You can give the sales clerk your number and ask her to call when the item has been marked down; I've done this, and usually, by the time I get the call, I can't even remember what I wanted.)

For Christmas, don't go overboard trying to keep things even. Christmas is not a competition. If you try to keep things equal for everyone, you'll get caught in a cycle of buying "one more thing"— and the dollars will steadily creep upward. Also, carefully consider how much you are comfortable spending for showers, weddings and birthdays. You needn't meet any certain expectation. Remember, it is the thought that counts. If you attach a heartfelt, thoughtful card to any gift, the true value skyrockets, no matter what's inside the paper wrapping.

A Cup of Financial Savvy

Ralph Waldo Emerson said, "Money often costs too much." When we always want more and become slaves to acquiring, we pay too high a price. How many of us work long hours to pay for gigantic houses we never have time to truly live in? Or stay awake nights, worried over debt and money issues? Do we define ourselves by what we have and try to impress? With credit card debt, foreclosures and bankruptcy at an all-time high, countless people are bound by spending and are paying the unfortunate price: loss of peace of mind, good credit ratings, even their homes. As Henry Fielding said, "If you make money your god, it will plague you like the devil."

When we look to money to give us what only God can, we are shortchanged every time.

Now don't get me wrong. Money is not evil. It is a tool God would have us use and manage wisely (see Matthew 25:14-30). The love of money is the problem. When we look to money to give us what only God can, we are shortchanged every time. Nothing—not stuff, not coffee, not even the local barista—can truly fill our cups . . . only God can. And will.

Questions to STIR

1. Think about your spending habits. Are there areas where you are a careless spender? Where might you be more resourceful when it comes to purchases?

2. Could you do a 40-day spending fast? What would you give up? What do you think you would gain?

3. Think about your car, clothes and the things you own. Do you look to material items to define you and give you worth? How might you look to God for your value?

Soul Sip Solutions

1. Clean out your closet and take a bag of clothes that don't fit anymore to Goodwill or some other donation center. How do

you feel? In what other area of your life can you simplify your material possessions and bless others at the same time?

2. Try to stop spending for two weeks. Plan meals from the food already in your freezer and find creative ways to make presents, if needed. What did you learn in those two weeks?

3. Take a close look at your finances. Are you living beyond your means? Where can you change spending habits to better honor God and regain financial health?

Reflection and Challenge

Do you have a budget? Do you need to pay off debt? Write down any problem areas you have, and then make a plan to stop careless spending (plan with your husband, if applicable).

_____

_____

_____

_____

_____

_____

_____

_____

_____

_____

_____

_____

_____

_____

_____

18

A FULL POT

Gratitude and Generosity

As we express our gratitude, we must never forget that the highest appreciation is not to utter words, but to live by them.
JOHN F. KENNEDY

Be thankful. Let the word of Christ dwell in you richly . . . as you sing psalms, hymns and spiritual songs with gratitude in your hearts to God.
COLOSSIANS 3:15-16

When you take that first sip of coffee in the morning, what do you feel? What are you thinking about? If you're anything like me, it's not much. My first sip, like a snuggle from a daughter who has crawled into my bed, is usually a sweet welcome to a new day. Later, as I wake up, my mind is abuzz with to-dos and responsibilities, but my first sip is fairly uneventful in the brainwave department. Sometimes, if the coffee is especially tasty, I'll look to see what kind of beans we have in the pantry; or if we're out of cream, I'll cowboy-up and drink it black. Otherwise, I just pour and imbibe.

I must admit, I don't think about the hands that nurtured the seedling coffee plants. I don't consider the workers who tended the coffee fields day in and day out; the many migrant families who harvested each berry by hand, sometimes for extremely low wages. I don't think of the processing, drying, hulling, cleaning, roasting, bagging, shipping and grinding. I usually don't even acknowledge my own husband's effort, who, before I ever wake, measures the beans and brews the blend, leaving a fresh pot at my fingertips as soon as I walk down the steps to the kitchen.

I take a lot for granted. I have many reasons to be grateful.

Even in something as simple as a sip of coffee, I am the recipient of a hundred blessings, poured selflessly into my cup.

Blessings Abound

Looking at my morning brew this way stirs up gratitude. How easy it is to overlook all the work and time that go into even a simple cup of coffee. Think about all the food we eat: the plum tomatoes, creamy avocados, tender artichokes and crunchy carrots in our lunchtime salad alone—that vitamin-packed bite represents lots of time, love and toil. Think about the clothes we wear—those favorite jeans started out as *cotton in a field somewhere*—and someone *made* the shirt on our backs.

Much of what we have today is the fruit and blessing of previous generations and others who've worked extremely hard. Think of our ancestors who toiled for the chance of a better life. Think about the teachers who helped us gain an education and the people who encouraged and loved us—coaches, family members, friends.

Make a habit of sharing what you are grateful for over dinner. The time together will foster family togetherness and an appreciation for blessings.

We have so much, and yet, sometimes it's easy to let the awareness of our true blessings slip beneath a haze of cushy dissatisfaction. Author Sarah Ban Breathnach and Oprah have both suggested the practice of keeping a gratitude journal. I've done this. It is a great exercise in paying careful attention to our myriad blessings. As the pages fill, blessings cannot be denied. Still, when filling in the blanks, I was often looking for the big-ticket blessing, the career promotion or the new car, instead of noting something simple—like a sip of coffee at the start of a new day.

Keeping a gratitude journal is a worthwhile practice and a good habit to build. It is a daily exercise in thankfulness—a conscious, mindful effort to appreciate every detail of our lives. Like a muscle that has not been challenged, it may take time to build a strong gratitude habit. But it is possible.

Pick up an orange at the grocery store, inhale the sweet citrus scent and silently thank God for the farmers who grew the oranges, the workers who picked, transported and stocked them. Hug your children and hold them tight. Thank God for their health, laughter, insights, love. Be conscious in celebrating and appreciating each moment, savoring every bite of life like melt-in-your-mouth chocolate cake. (It's even sweeter, and calorie-free!) Nurturing gratitude will help us to develop a deeper appreciation for our own daily blessings.

Giving Is a Blessing

Not long ago, Peyton and I went to Wal-Mart for a few craft supplies, birthday gifts and other nonessential odds and ends. We circled the store for about 20 minutes, picking up our items, and then headed for the checkout. The lines were crazy busy with people swarming like bees. Peyton ran up and down the rows, surveying which line was shortest, eventually directing me to an aisle behind a young mother with a toddler.

At first I didn't pay much attention to the woman in front of us. I chatted with Peyton, deflecting her requests for candy and gum like a goalie defending my pocketbook. After a while, however, I noticed that the line wasn't making any progress. As Peyton continued to survey the goodies available for purchase, I looked to see what was holding things up.

I noticed that the woman checking out was at best in her early twenties, and her baby was about 18 months. She appeared to have her mom with her too—and between them they had three shopping carts packed with food. The cashier had rung up most of her groceries and had begun, at her request, to check the balance after each item. The woman pointed to a few cans of peaches and said, "Do those." The cashier rang them up, and then checked the total. "Okay, now those," she said pointing to canned green beans. The process was slow—like watching bread rise. Finally, she said, "That's it. I'll have to leave the rest."

She handed over what seemed to be a credit card, and the cashier swiped it. It didn't go through. He tried again and then a third time. No luck.

"It should have more money than that," she said, her face flushed like a child who had put on too much of her mother's rouge. The woman looked at her mom. The older lady shrugged. "I guess I'll have to take some stuff out."

The two ladies began pulling items from their shopping bags— a bag of chips, a gigantic jar of pickles, cans of tuna. They seemed to be targeting the higher-priced items to bring the total down. The cashier subtracted each item and again checked the total.

It took me a while to figure out what was happening. This woman was on food stamps. (I guess they're not actually stamps anymore, but a debit-like card.) She was likely buying a month's supply of food—and had less money than expected. She was flustered and embarrassed.

I couldn't imagine spending all that time filling up three shopping carts (with a toddler in tow!) and then not having enough money. It was clear the older lady did not have the capacity to financially assist. My heart broke.

"I'll buy the rest of your groceries," I said on impulse to the young woman, motioning to the remaining items on the belt and the ones she had pulled from her bags.

"You're kidding," said the cashier.

"No, I'll buy them," I said. "Don't worry about it."

I wasn't sure what the total would be, but it didn't matter. This woman needed help, and I could give it.

"Are you sure?" the young woman asked.

"Yes," I said. "I'm sure."

Once her card finally cleared, I paid for the rest of her items.

"Thank you so much. If I ever see you again," she said, "I'll do the same for you."

"Not necessary," I said. "Everyone needs a little help sometimes."

After the woman and her mom left, the cashier shook his head in disbelief.

"Man, I've worked here two years and that's like the nicest thing I've ever seen," he said.

"I hope not," I replied.

"It is. People don't do stuff like that very much."

As we left the store, my feelings swirled like flavors in a blender. The encounter had given me an immediate, deep gratitude and appreciation for the abundance in my own life—and had opened my eyes to the need in my neighborhood. I was also surprised by the cashier's comment that "people don't do stuff like that very much." I found it hard to believe. I'd hope that anyone who had the funds and opportunity would have done the same. Most of all, I felt blessed for being able to help. The opportunity to give made me feel warm inside—like I had a cashmere scarf wrapped around my heart.

Plus, I'd made a positive impact on someone: Maybe it was the woman. Maybe it was the cashier. Or maybe it was my daughter. At some point, Peyton had turned her attention from the checkout candy and tuned in to what was happening. As we walked to our car, she looked up at me with a sideways, contemplative smile.

"That was really nice what you did, Mom."

I looked down at Peyton and smiled back. "Thanks," I replied. "I know you'd have done the same thing, if you could have. And that's what Jesus would have done too. Don't you think?"

A Cup of Gratitude and Generosity

Gratitude and giving go hand in hand. When we have hearts that are bursting with gratitude, it is easier for us to love, to forgive, to give—to share God's bounty.

There are many ways to give. We can give time, money or talents. We can also give words, encouraging others, lifting them up. We can give love in simple, everyday acts. Giving, in any capacity, can be scary, but it is an act of gratitude itself. Matthew 10:8 says, "Freely you have received, freely give." We can demonstrate gratitude for our blessings by giving to others when the opportunity presents itself.

We have a choice: We can hold tightly to what we have or embrace gratitude, trust God and use our lives to touch others. We can never outgive God (see James 1:17; Matthew 7:11). No matter what we do, He brings blessing back to us in abundance. That day at Wal-Mart, I was the recipient of the greater blessing: My heart was touched and I had the opportunity to model generosity for my daughter.

> *"Bring the whole tithe into the storehouse. . . .*
> *'Test me in this,' says the Lord Almighty, 'and see if I will not throw*
> *open the floodgates of heaven and pour out so much blessing*
> *you will not have enough room for it.'"* —MALACHI 3:10

I believe that giving generously keeps us under the umbrella of God's grace. Giving also opens our eyes to blessings we normally would not see—and I, for one, am filled with gratitude and joy for that.

Questions to STIR

1. Take stock of your life. What are you grateful for?

2. From a sip of coffee, to a pair of jeans, to your health, what are the things you might take for granted? Where might you lack gratitude?

3. Read Matthew 10:8 and think about giving. Do you give on a regular basis—of your time, talents or money? If not, why not? Does the idea of giving scare you? Why?

Soul Sip Solutions

1. Take Sarah Ban Breathnach's/Oprah's lead and keep a gratitude journal. Every day list all the blessings you can think of. Watch the abundance overflow.

2. What area of giving is hardest for you? Why? Where can you give—of time, talents or money—to bless others? Pick one way you can give, and do it this week.

3. It can be easy to adopt a scarcity mentality—thinking you might not have enough. From volunteering at a shelter to shopping at

a thrift store or driving through a needy part of town, what can you do to see your blessings in a different light?

Reflection and Challenge

Read Matthew 6:25-34. Giving is an expression of thankfulness toward God; we give because we have received. Do you agree with this statement? Why or why not? How have you been blessed by God? How can you begin to honor Him with your life and finances if you are not already doing so?

19

A SIP AT SUNRISE

Consistency and Resolve

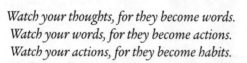

Watch your thoughts, for they become words.
Watch your words, for they become actions.
Watch your actions, for they become habits.
Watch your habits, for they become character.
Watch your character, for it becomes your destiny.
ANONYMOUS

I can do everything through him who gives me strength.
PHILIPPIANS 4:13

I love cream in my coffee. Well, actually, I like coffee in my cream. I like my coffee best when it moos. Yep. When it is whitish-colored, creamy and doesn't resemble java at all, then I'm in coffee heaven. Mmm. Tasty.

Only one problem: I have a hunch that maybe, just maybe, this isn't the healthiest way for me to drink my morning brew. The cream has a decent amount of saturated fat, and we all know that's not the best thing to ingest like clockwork each morning. Still, it's hard to resist. Nonfat milk and even the fat-free half-and-half are just *not* the same. I like the clog-your-arteries kind.

Recently, I decided to give up cream after a physical showed that my cholesterol numbers were way up. Aside from coffee cream, I don't eat much fatty stuff and am generally a healthy eater. Stress, and not enough exercise, may have been the culprit, but I figured the cream wasn't helping. So it had to go.

I had one big "good-bye to creamer" cup, savoring every slurp. Then I tossed the carton and resolved to change my ways.

Day One: I drank my coffee black and figured myself a coffee connoisseur, someone who cannot "pollute" the brew with creamers, sweeteners and other such fluff. I tried to savor the true flavor of the beans but eventually decided I liked "polluted" coffee.

Day Two: Decided that if I was a true connoisseur, I might need to switch out my month-old mega can for some specialty beans. Opened a new bag, ground them up and watched the coffee maker dispense the drink. It was okay. Still not as good as my creamy concoction, but I suffered through.

Day Three: Got a nonfat latte after I dropped my kids at school. Figured the nonfat milk would not contribute to my cholesterol. While in the coffee shop, saw a French press and decided maybe *that* was the key to good coffee. Bought it.

Day Four: Ditched the coffee maker and tried to make my brew in the French press. What resulted was a grittier, grindier brew that left black specks in my teeth. Dumped it out and went upstairs to floss.

Day Five: Made a cup of "heart healthy" green tea—skipping my brew altogether. Not the same. Sigh.

Day Six: My husband had purchased a new pint of half-and-half, so I snuck a teensy bit. My coffee was just sort of tan. Was semi-satisfied and semi-guilt ridden.

Day Seven: Made my coffee with lots of cream. Delicious. Downed every last sip. Then chugged a "cholesterol reducing" yogurt drink with plant sterols and went for a walk. Figured there had to be a way to compromise. Changing my coffee habit wasn't as easy as I thought it'd be.

Character Building Disciplines

I'm still working on changing my coffee habit. Most days I drink it black (and enjoy it), but I occasionally cave, indulging like a L'Oreal girl—"because I'm worth it." Changing a habit is not easy. Building good practices starts with good choices rooted in our values. Ultimately, whether drinking more water, exercising regularly or changing your diet, you've got to be clear on the why of your motivation or, like a car without gas, you won't get very far.

My reason for eliminating cream was to help lower my cholesterol. While this is a valid reason, given the opportunity to stir in some cream, I'd take a walk or trade out a hamburger later in the day and still imbibe. Aside from knowing I'd be healthier, I had no vested interest in changing my habits; I liked cream in my coffee too much. However, finally facing the reality that higher cholesterol contributes to the risk of stroke—and a stroke could leave me physically and mentally impaired *or dead*—my motivation got serious. I thought about not being here for my daughters and finally canned the cream.

> Cholesterol comes from two sources: your body and the food you eat. About 75% of blood cholesterol is made in the liver and other cells. —AMERICANHEART.ORG[1]

When establishing—or changing—any habit, it's essential to get the motivation from our brain to our heart. Make it personal. If you want to lose weight—simply hoping to fit back into your "skinny" jeans may not do the trick because you can always buy different jeans. However, if you want to shed pounds and get fit so that you have more energy to keep up with your kids on the ski slopes, that might be more of a true catalyst for change.

No matter the goal, establishing good habits consists of a series of smaller decisions and strategic action. Good choices are the little steps that add up to big change. Choosing to eat an apple instead of a cookie just takes a bit more resolve. Drinking more water may mean keeping a few bottles in your car or a pitcher on your desk. Establishing a practice of reading with your children before bedtime might mean doing the dishes after they go to sleep. You get the idea.

If you tend to scroll through "attempts to change" like a man with a remote control, then I think progressive rewards are in order. Call it positive reinforcement, incentive, whatever—give yourself treats as you make progress. I used M&M treats with my younger daughter when she was potty training. Now I use a similar method to retrain myself in good behaviors.

For example, when I want a new outfit, if I rationalize: *I'll work out for a month, then I'll buy it,* I may exercise a few times, but I'll never follow through. A month is just too long; I can't stick to it. However, if after one workout I buy a lipstick, three workouts get me the shirt, six workouts deliver the pants, nine workouts the shoes, and twelve workouts the accessories (now on sale!), then I have the motivation to keep at it. While monetary motivators work—the incentive may be any kind of treat. Once a routine is established, you won't need to continue external motivators; the action will become its own reward.

A Healthy Example

Another help when establishing a good habit (or breaking a bad one) is to follow the example of someone who has her priorities in order. My friend Carolyn is just such a person. In college, she never watched television in the afternoon; after class she would go straight to her room and study. Those habits paid off in good grades and time to relax in the evening. These days, her personal discipline translates into consistent exercise and a healthy diet. She inspires me to hit the gym and make veggie stir-fry. Her example challenges me to do better. Surrounding yourself with people who are successful in your area of desired growth gives a boost to your own efforts.

This line of thinking follows the "quality in, quality out" principle. Set yourself up for success by finding heart-level motivation, by rewarding progress and by surrounding yourself with the positive: good examples, healthy food choices, quality books, and the like. Determination alone, like toddlers coordinating their own outfits, won't always produce the result you want. If I want to make good food choices, but I keep coffee-flavored Haägen-Dazs in the freezer, at some point I'll think, *Haägen-Dazs is a darn good choice.* If low-fat lemon yogurt is my only option, then it helps me make a better decision.

Developing good habits and discipline, like constructing the Empire State Building out of Legos, can be a long process and a lot of work. You do it bit by bit (see Isaiah 28:10). Yet, in life, everything we do adds up. It's true—what you think becomes what you say; what you say becomes what you do; what you do (repeatedly) forms habits; and your habits—good or bad—shape your life.

A Cup of Consistency and Resolve

Not long ago, my husband and I were lying in bed watching the late-night news. I was thinking about what motivates people—about the common denominator in success. My mind churned, but I wasn't coming up with anything concrete. So I asked my husband.

"Pete, do you have any profound thoughts on consistency and resolve?"

He paused, snorted like a horse and started to laugh. "Honey, you should know me better than that."

The next day, I asked my hairdresser, Kim, the same question. "Hmmm, that's a tough one," she said.

It is a tough one. If I could bottle and sell discipline and consistency, I'd be more successful than Bill Gates; but I can't and I'm not. The answer lies in only one place.

When my daughter Peyton turned nine, she had a big party, and my sister-in-law, Lori, flew in from out of town to join the festivities. When she walked in the door, my husband and I were astonished. She had lost a significant amount of weight and had a healthy, radiant glow. She looked amazing.

"Wow, you look great! What's your secret?" I asked.

She smiled and said, "I just gave it to God. After trying and trying, I just couldn't do it in my own power. I looked to Him for strength—and it was really hard at first, but then the weight just started to come off."

With every thought, every moment, every donut hole, we must look to God and follow His example.

She didn't do it in her own strength. She looked to God. Between you and me, doesn't this just seem so easy to say and so tough to do? Just what does that mean exactly? The Bible is chock-full of references to the Lord being our strength: "Those who hope in the LORD will renew their strength" (Isaiah 40:31); "The joy of the LORD is your strength" (Nehemiah 8:10); "The LORD is my strength and my song" (Psalm 118:14). But how do you take God's strength and apply it to the mundane coffee-cream decisions of life?

The answer lies in Jesus. Following the right example, like one-way signs on a busy highway, is critical to our wellbeing. There is no better example to look to than Jesus. First Chronicles 16:11 says, "Look to the LORD and his strength; seek his face always." Seek His face always. That's the key. With every thought, every moment, every donut hole, we must look to God and follow His example. The more we seek Him, the more we will understand His character and our motivations. And if we truly seek and surrender, it can transform us—in every way. "Set your minds on things above, not earthly things" (Colossians 3:2). Look up, not in. Our motivation must be rooted in God's purpose and strength—not our own. Psalm 18:32 says, "It is God who arms me with strength and makes my way perfect." That's consistency, resolve and transformation just waiting for us to say *yes*.

Questions to STIR

1. Think of a habit you'd like to change. What is holding you back? What is your true motivation for change? Is it rooted in your heart or brain?

2. What does it mean for you to fully trust and hope in Jesus? Read Psalm 20 and think about what it would look like to fully trust God. How might you look to Him and receive His help in developing good habits, consistency and resolve?

3. Think of people who look to you. What example do they see?

Soul Sip Solutions

1. If you are trying to establish a new habit (or lose a bad one) think of a way to reward yourself with little treats as you make progress. Try it for a week and see how you do.

2. This month read a psalm each day, with the number of the
    psalm corresponding with the day of the month. For example,
    read Psalm 1 on May 1, Psalm 2 on May 2, and so on until May
    27, when you read Psalm 27. Pay careful attention to the refer-
    ences to God being your strength. Pray that God would be your
    strength in all areas of your life.

3. Who are the people who provide a positive example to you? Do
    you have any women you look to for guidance? If so, where do
    they get their strength? Ask them. If you don't know any
    women mentors, how might you find one? Cultivate positive
    role models.

Reflection and Challenge

Think of a time when you tried to change a habit and failed. Ask
God to give you the strength to try again. Journal your thoughts
and your progress below.

_____

_____

_____

_____

_____

_____

_____

_____

_____

_____

_____

_____

_____

COFFEE BREAK
WITH JANE

Dear Moms,

When my children were small, we played a favorite game at the dinner table. Each person would take a turn describing three things they were thankful for. Often their answers revealed the wonder of God's creation (fuzzy caterpillars or snow-frosted trees); but sometimes they revealed the depth of their heart (a hurt soothed by a friend or an unexpected act of generosity). I learned a lot about my children during those times, and hopefully planted the seeds of gratitude.

As they grew older, it got easier to dwell on negative thoughts—just read the paper or watch the nightly news: a school shooting, a friend's overdose, a neighbor's suicide.

The apostle Paul must have known our tendency to dwell on despair when he issued this challenge: "Whatever is true, whatever is noble, whatever is right, whatever is pure, whatever is lovely, whatever is admirable—if anything is excellent or praiseworthy—think about such things" (Philippians 4:8).

A few years ago, my father was diagnosed with macular degeneration of the eyes. The news was devastating. Once a star athlete, a decorated Marine and successful coach, he has given up most of the activities he's loved all his life, fishing and golf in particular.

Dad has always gone to church, but he was never one to read the Bible. Now that it has gotten hard for him to read, my mom has read the entire Bible to him! He never would have sat still long enough before. Isn't that just like God to turn what seems like a tragedy into a blessing we are thankful for?!

We choose what we dwell on. When we choose to dwell on what is good (like those times around the dinner table), our disposition softens. We begin to appreciate the small delights of God's creation (caterpillars) and the immense wisdom of His ways (slowing us down for what is important). We become thankful. Contentment flows from a grateful heart. We become rivers of living water blessing others.

Jane Norton

2 0

SPILLS HAPPEN

Forgiveness

The weak can never forgive. Forgiveness is the attribute of the strong.
MAHATMA GANDHI

Forgive as the Lord forgave you.
COLOSSIANS 3:13

The roads were snowy, ice packed and slippery. As I drove, I felt like I was in a North Pole snow globe, with light snow falling all around me and winter white covering every surface I could see. The street signs were barely visible, most covered completely with snow that had frozen to them during the night. And it was cold. The temperature was in the twenties, with a biting wind that froze your nose hair the instant you stepped outside.

I'd left the house extra early, allowing time to navigate the frozen slip-and-slide and reach my appointment on time. Surprisingly, traffic was light, and though it was slow going, I arrived half an hour early. I'd waited several months to meet this physician, and as a new medical sales rep, I wanted to make a good impression. I'd spent hours preparing my talk and presentation materials, rehearsing my sales pitch numerous times in the bathroom mirror. I was wearing my very best suit. I was prepared. Nothing, not the snowy roads nor cold weather could deter me. I was going to have a great meeting.

When I drove up, however, the office was dark. So with time to kill, I decided to drive across the street and warm up with a latte.

The coffee shop was eerily empty—even the most loyal customers had stayed home this morning. All except me.

"Hi," said the barista. "What can I get you?"

"I'll have a nonfat latte," I said. "Medium."

We chatted about the weather, and then, with drink in hand, I thanked her and made my way to the door.

"Have a nice day," she said.

"I will," I replied. But as I stepped outside, my foot slipped on a sheet of ice. Instantly, I flung my arms into the air to stabilize myself. The lid came off my latte and—in what seemed like a slow-motion crash—I fell onto the ice, my latte splashing all over me. (Most of it was in my hair.) In an instant, I went from confident and pulled-together to embarrassed and drenched in hot milk. The barista, who witnessed my tumble through the glass door, rushed out to help.

"Oh my gosh," she said. "I'm so sorry. I noticed that was slippery when I opened the shop. Are you hurt? Oh . . . you need a new latte."

What I needed was a new suit and a blow dryer. But now I didn't have time. Holding back tears, I got up and made my way to the car. What I saw in the rearview mirror made me want to collapse in a heap of despair. My hair was matted with milk, my mascara smeared. I was a wreck. I needed latte-crash triage—and quick.

I licked a tissue and wiped the black smudges from under my eyes. I pulled a small comb from my purse and tried to fix my hair, but it was impossible. After much effort, I pulled my hair into a tight ponytail. The milk was already drying (or freezing), leaving me with a mane of crusty, hard, uncooked spaghetti with a sour-milk odor. Not pretty. I wanted to go home, but I had to keep the appointment— and so I drove back across the street and walked into the office.

Ending "The Blame Game"

As I drove home later that morning, I started to get angry. Really angry. I wondered why, if the barista had noticed the ice, she hadn't put some salt down or shoveled it away. Why didn't she warn me or better secure the lid on my latte? As the questions raced through my mind, I began to blame her for my fall. She was the scapegoat for my frustration and fury. But really, she wasn't to blame. She could have warned me; perhaps she planned to and forgot. Maybe she wanted to clear the sidewalk but didn't have rock salt or a shovel. Ultimately, it was an accident—neither her fault nor mine, but I wanted someone to take responsibility for my hurt feelings.

Guilt is the gift that keeps on giving. —Jewish Proverb

Events like this happen all the time. I can think of instances with my husband when I've felt wronged—not maliciously or intentionally—but I wanted someone to blame, my internal conversation revealing a hard wall of pride: *I deserve better than this. This is not what I signed up for. How dare he?* But this kind of thought process is like walking uphill on a treadmill; it wears you out and doesn't get you anywhere. It just builds negative feelings, and unless dealt with, like burping fish oil, it keeps coming up again and again—and really stinks.

The solution, of course, requires a little perspective and a whole lot of humility. Perspective comes when you step back from the situation and try to view it from an outsider's point of view. Often when people hurt or wrong us, they do not mean to do it. Other times, when we *feel* wronged, we are choosing to feel that way, placing blame on others so that we don't have to face our own failures, attitudes and imperfections. I've hurt people's feelings before *and had no idea* I'd said or done something offensive. Sometimes we don't think about how our actions or words may be received by another.

Humility helps us wash the sour latte out of our own hair before we try to shampoo another's crusty mop. Humility helps us see that the world does not revolve around us. I admit, I like to think there is something revolving around me, but usually it's just a bug attracted to the stench of my pride. When I get on my *I deserve better* kick, no one benefits. My relationships suffer, and I suffer. Yet, I sink into pride like my spoon sinks into yogurt—quickly and most every day. It is easy to think that pride is strength and humility is weakness, but really, it's the other way around. Pride looks out for Number One. Humility sees the Big Picture and is unassuming and gentle. Humility realizes that we are all on the same team and takes responsibility because it is the right thing to do.

Lessons in Humility and Forgiveness

God gives me little lessons in humility and forgiveness all the time. It's not always fun, but I have to say, the Big Guy gets His point across. A few years ago, I bought a new car, a shining silver beauty. It was just a couple months old when my husband backed into it— in our garage. He had been out of town, so I'd pulled right into the middle, taking up both spaces. When he got home, assuming that I'd parked on my side, he backed right into my car, crushing the taillight and denting the back.

"How did you not see it?" I asked him incredulously.

"I dunno. I didn't see it. I'm sorry."

Pete didn't say, "Your car was in the middle of the garage, it's your fault." He just apologized. But I didn't forgive. I continued to bring it up, reminding him of *his* error, placing all the blame on him. "How did you not see it?" I asked again and again.

Not long after, Pete and I were at a wedding with friends, and I was the designated driver. When it was time to go, we all climbed into Pete's truck and I proceeded to back out of the parking space. Then I heard a crunch. I had been looking behind me, but still, I'd backed right into someone's car. We got out to survey the damage, and I couldn't believe my eyes: The car I'd backed into was the exact make and model as my own. And the owners were in the car. But instead of scolding or blaming me for the error, they (and especially Pete) were extremely gracious.

☕ *People are more important than stuff. Accidents happen, and placing blame does not accomplish anything.*

Later, the insurance claim revealed that I'd done the exact damage to the stranger's car that Pete had done to mine. Same accident. Same car. Same damage. (And you don't think God has a sense of humor?!) What I realized once I was in the driver's seat was that from a certain angle you can't see my car when backing up in Pete's truck. The truck is too high. Not only did I now understand Pete's point of view but, after seeing how gracious a stranger had been to me, I was ashamed that I hadn't extended the same grace to my husband. After all, it was only a car. A little humility and forgiveness would have gone a long way in strengthening my marriage and preventing hurt feelings, rather than creating ill will.

A Cup of Forgiveness

I'd like to say the car incident is the only lesson I've had in humility and forgiveness. It's not. Not even close. However, I am learning to keep perspective, remembering that people are more important than stuff. Accidents happen, and placing blame doesn't accomplish anything. I'm learning that forgiveness sometimes means choosing to overlook or to release a wrong even when I don't feel like it. Forgiveness does not come easy for me, or for most people. It requires letting go of pride and my *I don't deserve this* attitude. This often feels like sawing my ego in half with a dull butter knife—or having my pride trampled in Pamplona. And though painful, it's good for me. The pains may be similar to the ones my kids feel in their legs—growing pains.

The Bible talks a lot about forgiveness. Forgiveness is the reason for Jesus' incarnation and sacrifice—for all our wrongdoing. Now, obviously, Jesus would not have chosen the horrific suffering of crucifixion if there were any other way. Just the evening before His crucifixion, He prayed, "My Father, if it is possible, may this cup be taken from me. Yet not as I will, but as you will" (Matthew 26:39). He did not want to die, but was obedient, even to death. What would have happened to us—and the course of human history—had He decided, *I didn't sign up for this. I deserve better than this?*

Thinking of His example, attitude and monumental sacrifice helps me be humble and forgive when I don't want to. Seeing the forgiveness that was extended to me helps me extend it to others—and often, once I have, it feels like a thousand helium balloons lifting off, carrying the resentment and despair far away.

Colossians 3:13 tells us to "bear with each other and forgive whatever grievances [we] may have against one another." That's good advice. Think of how many friendships, relationships and marriages would be saved if we all learned to forgive. It's not easy, but then you know what they say: *Nothing worthwhile ever is.*

Questions to STIR

1. Think of an instance when you felt wronged or offended. Did you assign blame? Do you still harbor resentment? What can you do to release anger and forgive?

2. How do you define "humble"? Do you see humility as weakness or strength? Why?

3. Psalm 103:3 says God forgives all our sins. How does this free you to love yourself and others? How does it give you strength?

Soul Sip Solutions

1. If you are harboring resentment or offense toward anyone, pray and ask God to give you strength to forgive them.

2. Ask God to show you areas in your life where pride may be an issue. Ask God to help you change your attitudes and ways.

3. The next time you have the opportunity to feel hurt or offended, choose to be humble. Act and react in love.

Reflection and Challenge

If you are married, take a few moments to reflect on your marriage. Are there instances where you could have been more humble or extended forgiveness for the sake of the relationship? Write some of these below. Consider writing your husband a letter expressing your love and support of him, asking forgiveness for past wrongs.

_____

_____

_____

_____

_____

_____

_____

21

THE JITTERS

Trust

Only when we are no longer afraid do we begin to live.
DOROTHY THOMPSON

Trust in the LORD with all your heart.
PROVERBS 3:5

Reading a parenting magazine stresses me out. Tucked in between articles on how to get your children to eat veggies and nap on schedule is information on SIDS, dangerous toys, allergic reactions, childhood diseases, and more. After reading about possible choking hazards, which seem to encompass every item in my house, I feel tense. Reading about autism and child molesters quickens my breathing and skyrockets my blood pressure. "Information" designed to prevent disaster fills me with anxiety and fear.

How can a mom sleep with infinite scenarios for disaster spinning in her head? I certainly cannot. *What if my kids choke on popcorn while watching a movie? What if they accidentally ingest something poisonous? What if they get hit by a car or are kidnapped? What if I am not there to help?* I live with perpetual, fearful "what if . . ." scenarios.

One day the "what ifs" hit a record crescendo. I have returned home from shopping and while making a pot of "pick me up" coffee and putting away groceries, my typically inquisitive toddler investigates the supermarket treasures. Soon I detect the telltale odor of nail polish and discover my daughter sucking on a bottle I'd just purchased—a tiny bit of color oozing from the top. Panic bells start to ring. I feel sick.

"My daughter just drank a bottle of nail polish!" I cry to Poison Control.

📖 *How do you care and not worry? Is it possible to*
worry without suffocating joy?

"Is there any polish in her mouth? Can you tell how much? Did she really drink the whole bottle?" the woman asks.

"Well, the lid is not totally off," I confess. "So I'm not sure she really drank any . . . but she might have." My more rational self suspects that she has not ingested anything—but I need reassurance. After a series of related questions, the woman advises me to watch for any irritation around her mouth and to call with further concerns.

Rather than feeling relieved, I spend the afternoon in the land of "What if?" *What if she really had ingested nail polish? What if I hadn't noticed? What if, what if, what if?* I am physically and emotionally exhausted from anxious thoughts. No need for an afternoon cup of coffee: I already have the jitters.

Worthless Worry

How do you care and not worry? Or worry without suffocating joy? Fear is a normal reaction to a perceived threat. When we feel threatened—whether physically or emotionally—our bodies have a natural *fight or flight* reaction, gearing up to deal with the circumstances at hand. In some situations, fear is a good thing. It engenders healthy respect and reasonable caution when dealing with potentially harmful situations. It helps us moms protect our kids, guiding us in simple acts of caution and protection: cutting a hot dog into small pieces, teaching our little ones to look for cars before they cross the street, keeping cleaning products out of reach. However, fear becomes abnormal when it is—like my nail polish incident—distorted or exaggerated in proportion to a situation.

It is good to mentally prepare, but avoid forecasting worst-case scenarios. If left to the horror film reeling in my head, I envision a zillion ways my kids might be hurt, or my life might fall apart: every sneeze could develop into the bird flu, a minor cut into a staph infection, an ache into bone cancer. It sounds ridiculous, and it is. Fear and worry paralyze me like I've been dipped in liquid nitrogen, instantly fragile, breakable, and cold—not the warm, attentive mom I want to be.

The root of fear is a lack of knowledge. When we know and understand the statistics, the facts, and the truth, we realize that most of what we worry about never happens. We lose precious moments of life when gripped with worry—crushing the potential beauty of our lives like a wildflower in a child's grip. We are butterflies caught in a pickle jar, unable to fly; we frantically flutter and spin in a disoriented panic, unaware there is no lid—and if only we were to look up, we could be free.

God of All: The Known and the Unknown

I am no stranger to fear. I know it well. When Peyton was five (long after the nail polish incident), she started to shuffle and drag her feet. She seemed disoriented at times, once falling off the toilet, once walking into a mailbox on the way to the park. She would throw up in the morning for no apparent reason and had a light appetite. I wasn't sure what was going on, but my *mom* intuition told me things were not right. However gloom and doom I tended to be, I did not come close to forecasting the diagnosis: Peyton had a brain tumor. What started as a quick visit to the doctor on the way to the zoo turned into a CAT scan, an MRI and a life-changing talk with a pediatric oncologist and a neurosurgeon.

Peyton was admitted to the hospital, and I was gripped with fear. Terrified does not adequately describe the foreboding and dread that surrounded me like deadly carbon monoxide, robbing my lungs of oxygen, leaving me immobile, crippled and confused. I was taunted by questions, fearful of the answers: *Was the tumor cancerous? Would she suffer neurologic loss? Would she live?*

Peyton was in the hospital for a month, undergoing four brain surgeries and more tests and pokes than I can count. During this time, I began to understand how worry can destroy you, tugging and nagging like a stranger dragging you into dark places you don't want—or need—to go. Stress zapped my body. I had been breast-feeding Morgan, but my milk instantly dried up. I lost weight, my cheekbones betraying my anxious state. Friends commented that I looked shorter—and I was, physically weighed down with worry for my child.

When we worry, we play God. Worrying is not trusting that God can handle our problems. Worry takes outcomes from His hands and places them into our own where we become powerless small gods of worry. For weeks I prayed but clung to fear. Ultimately, I surrendered and gave God total control.

Trust is a choice—every moment of every day. It is a scary world we live in, no doubt about it. Bad things can happen. But this I learned: Trusting God is the only option. Living through a worst-case scenario showed me that God can handle it—all my stuff, my kids, me. He does care for us—and He is with us—always. Peyton's ordeal gave me the perspective to see how useless my magazine reading, news watching, nail polish reacting worry was. God is the God of all—the known and the unknown. We must trust Him with absolutely everything: Fretting about what may be robs us of the joy of living.

A Cup of Trust

I'd be lying to say I don't worry anymore. I do. Trusting God is not a one-time act; it is choosing to look to Him in every opportunity; for every want, concern or fear. Sometimes I fail. Some days I don't completely trust—or I'll worry that the outcome of a certain test or situation won't be what I want. At these times, worry blindfolds my heart and mind, holding me captive until I release it all to God.

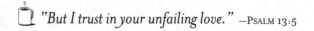 *"But I trust in your unfailing love."* —Psalm 13:5

Being moms gives us lots of worries, but also the opportunity to build our trust in the Lord. We care; we love our kids. We want what's best for them. Some fear and worry is normal, but it is also important to understand that God gives them His best. He has entrusted them to us to love, but we must ultimately acknowledge they belong to Him, and trust Him back. "I have believed, and am convinced that he is able to guard what I have entrusted to him" (2 Timothy 1:12).

Proverbs 3:5-6 is one of my favorite Bible passages. I've quoted it before, but it is worth repeating: "Trust in the LORD with all your heart and lean not on your own understanding; in all your ways acknowledge him, and he will make your paths straight." Trust the Lord with all your heart—that means with everything we've got. And "lean not on your own understanding"—for me that's key. My own understanding is zippo. I don't see the big picture; my finite brain cannot grasp all that an omniscient God knows and how He works. I don't understand even an inkling of why bad things happen, but I know that He can redeem them. We just need to release our fear and trust in His goodness (see Jeremiah 17:7).

Unexpected things will happen; that's life. Taking responsibility to make sure that safeguards are in place is a good thing, but then we need to *live*. Don't waste time with worst-case scenarios. (And definitely stay away from the Internet if you're thinking about Googling symptoms or statistics: That is the front door to a fear circus.) Just remember: Most of what we worry about never happens. Live in the now—giving your children the best of every moment. That's what trust is all about.

Questions to STIR

1. Do you have a tendency toward excessive worry? If so, how much of what you worry about has come to fruition? Is fear holding you back from a full life?

2. It takes a lot of courage to be a mom. How can you "trust in the Lord with all your heart"? What would this look like? How would it change your daily life with your kids?

3. First Chronicles 5:20 says, "He answered their prayers, because they trusted in him." Do you trust God to deal with all your stuff—every fear, every detail? How might you trust Him more?

Soul Sip Solutions

1. Read Psalm 34:4. Write a list of everything you worry about. Now, one by one, give these to God in prayer. Ask Him to help deliver you from the fears—and details—of your life.

2. Take a look around your house and think about your rules and precautions. Have you taken appropriate action to put safeguards in place? Do you avoid unnecessary risks? If so, relax.

3. Say no to excessive worry and fear. It has no place in your life. (It might feel weird, but audibly rebuke unwarranted anxiety and fear.) How do you feel after doing that?

Reflection and Challenge

Think about your daily life. Do you lose time worrying about the future? If so, make a conscious decision to give every detail to God as it bubbles up in your brain. Try it for a day, then take a few moments to journal your experience.

_____

_____

_____

_____

_____

_____

_____

_____

_____

_____

_____

_____

_____

22

PERCOLATING PEARLS

Wisdom

Never mistake knowledge for wisdom. One helps you make a living;
the other helps you make a life.
SANDRA CAREY

This is my prayer: that your love may abound more and more in knowl-
edge and depth of insight, so that you may be able to discern what is best.
PHILIPPIANS 1:9-10

"Hey, Celeste, how are you?" asked my friend Lynne, when I answered
the phone.

"I'm great. How 'bout you?" I replied, as I tossed a load of laundry
into the dryer.

"Good. Nothing much new with me. I was just calling to see
if you had time to meet for coffee."

"Sure," I said. "When were you thinking?"

"Today. Can you do today?"

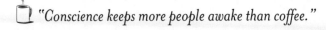

"Conscience keeps more people awake than coffee."

—AUTHOR UNKNOWN

Noting the urgency in her voice, I decided to postpone my
chores and meet her that afternoon.

When I got to the coffee shop, she was waiting. This was not like her; she was usually late. Something was definitely amiss.

Sure enough, as soon as I got my vanilla latte and sat down, Lynne erupted, a tearful Mount Vesuvius.

"I don't know what to do," she said, recounting her troubles.

"Yeah, that's tough," I empathized.

"What do you think?" she asked. "If you were in my situation, what would you do?"

Advice: Consider the Source

Advice. We give it, take it, want it. When I was a child, my dad would jokingly say, "Advice is only as good as what you pay for it." Maybe that's true. But you can ante up a whole lot of green and still get some bad advice. So what is the source of true wisdom? And where do we gain the insights that guide us on the right path through life? Some knowledge is a result of our own experience; like the oyster, we learn from all that life sends us, transforming grit and adversity into pearls of wisdom. Some "smarts" we inherit from our parents, grandparents, mentors, counselors and friends. But all wisdom ultimately comes from God (see James 1:5).

When you were a kid, didn't you wonder how your parents knew things you didn't think they would or could know? I used to wonder how my mom had the inside track on me; it seemed as if she had some sort of superpower X-ray vision into my brain. Funny, I now have those powers with my girls.

"Mom, do you know who my favorite singer is?" Peyton asks.

"Hannah Montana," I reply.

"Yep. Well, do you know my *new* favorite color?"

"It was purple, now it's blue—a greenish blue."

"Hey, how'd you know that?" she asks, amazed.

"I know because I'm your mom," I tell her.

What is so obvious to me now, which I didn't realize as a child, is that my parents used to be just like me. They used to pretend that "hot" lava was flowing over the ground; they used to avoid cracks in the sidewalk so that they didn't "break someone's back"; they fought with siblings over toys and clothes—just like my kids do now.

Insight and wisdom gained over a lifetime help us to be better parents and better people; help us know when to talk and when to listen, when to act and when to wait, when to encourage, challenge or discipline. However, experience is only part of the equation. Our own experience only goes so far. So we look to others for guidance.

We seek answers to life's dilemmas, often because we are not sure what to do or because we are hesitant to take full responsibility for what may prove to be an unwise decision. I have asked many a friend for her opinion, but I am often hesitant to dispense advice. What if the advice I offer isn't a "fit" for her situation? What if my advice results in a less-than-ideal outcome? How would I feel? What would be learned and who would be responsible?

Perspicacity Perks

Okay. Let's see if we can get the pearls percolating. The definition of "perspicacity" is (pick one): (A) An accumulation of sweat in your armpits; (B) An ancient coffee known for its ability to enhance brain function; (C) Discernment; understanding clearly; (E) A fancy term for the smarty-pants attitude from your five-year-old; (F) The sticky stuff left on your fingers after you eat a fruit roll-up.

Didn't know you were going to have an SAT review today? (Well, you can't say you didn't learn anything from this book.) Perspicacity is "C," discernment. Discernment—knowing something intuitively or understanding clearly—is key in giving advice. Discernment helps us listen to what is not being said as much as to what is being said, and to see the truth of a situation. It is having wisdom, and knowing when and how to apply it. When I was with my friend, I chose to opt out of the Dear Abby role; I encouraged her but didn't try to "fix" it. As a parent, I do the same thing. Sometimes, depending on the situation, I give advice; but more often, I give guidance, the facts as I see them, and ask my kids what they think Jesus would do. I try to be discerning—reading between the *whines*—looking beyond words and actions to the heart, and encourage my children to do the same.

Sandra Carey's quote about knowledge and wisdom really hits the target: *Knowledge helps us make a living; wisdom helps us make a life.* Wisdom is common sense applied judiciously, weaving meaning and purpose together on life's loom, with a resultant rich, rewarding tapestry.

Much of what I know I learned from my parents. To this day, I may look to them for guidance and advice. Yet, I've built upon that understanding by also looking to God, who gives knowledge and wisdom without the element of human error.

The more we become like-minded with God through His Word, the more insightful we can be with each other (see Philippians 2:5). God guides us in what is right and true when we align our hearts and minds with Him. We become better parents, friends, coworkers and leaders when we follow the guidance given in Colossians 3:16: "Let the word of Christ dwell in you richly as you teach and admonish one another with all wisdom, and as you sing psalms, hymns and spiritual songs with gratitude in your hearts to God."

A Cup of Wisdom

There are all sorts of proclaimed authorities in the world today. Self-help books abound. People ask for advice—and often give it unsolicited. So it is imperative that we judge all "truth" against God's Word and His wisdom. This is especially important when we are in a position of trust in giving advice and guidance to our children, coworkers, family and friends. Sometimes the best advice is simply the example of our own life lived in a way that honors God.

It is imperative that we judge all "truth" against God's Word and His wisdom.

When we sit down to share a cup of our personal perspicacity with another, may we do so knowing that we have first sipped a cup of wisdom with God through His Word. May we allow God to instruct us in His perfect ways. Then when we have occasion to "share our pearls," we may have the confidence of David, when he prayed in Psalm 19:14, "May the words of my mouth and the meditation of my heart be pleasing in your sight, O LORD, my Rock and my Redeemer."

Questions to STIR

1. When you run into tough times, where do you turn for advice? Do you look to God for guidance?

2. What are your sources of wisdom? If it is the nightly news, or talk shows, or anything else other than God—it is likely to be flawed. Only God offers rock-solid truth and guidance.

3. Read Proverbs 9:10. What does it mean when it says that "the fear of the Lord is the beginning of wisdom"?

Soul Sip Solutions

1. Next time someone asks you for advice, try to use discernment in your response, and if applicable, direct them toward God's example and wisdom rather than your own.

2. When your children look to you, what example do they see? (They are getting smarter by the day, Mom.) How can you continually gain wisdom to better lead and guide them?

3. Just for fun, use the word "perspicacious" in your next conversation with your husband. Is he impressed or confuddled? (My husband jokingly tells me to use the "abridged" version of my vocabulary when talking with him. ☺)

Reflection and Challenge

Spend a few moments looking up verses related to "wisdom" in your Bible. Write down the ones that speak to your heart.

_____

_____

_____

_____

_____

_____

COFFEE BREAK
WITH TAMY

Dear Moms,

My name is Blessed.

Recently, I was privileged to meet Dr. James Dobson, founder and chairman of the board of Focus on the Family. After exchanged greetings, he asked a question that shot straight to my heart: "Do you complain about your children?"

The question was surprising, but the conviction that followed was more shocking. I'd never identified myself as a complainer, but the truth was, I complained inwardly every time motherhood and marriage commanded things I did not anticipate. That day, I, Complainer, laid my heart at Jesus' feet and begged Him for a sacrificial heart like His.

Then, while reading Exodus 16:7, I discovered a promise God makes to all of us: "In the morning you will see the glory of the LORD." When the Israelites were wandering in the desert, God provided them manna from heaven. As instructed, they gathered as much as they needed each morning. Some days an individual's portion was great; and other days little; but each day God's provision was abundant. Our Lord still gives us manna each day and reveals His glory in the morning! I'm inclined to be a complainer and call upon my old companions pride, discontent and self-centered; but when I meet with the Lord each morning, He reveals His glory and teaches me His truth from His Word.

In John 6:35, Jesus tells us, "I am the bread of life. He who comes to me will never go hungry." He fills my cup with just what I need and sends me faithful companions like grace, wisdom and love. *Then He calls me Blessed* so that I can bless those He entrusts to me.

My prayer is that your cup will be filled each day with the Spirit of God, and you will be thrilled as you witness the glory of the Lord with the dawn of each new day.

Sincerely,

Tamy Elam

23

DELICIOUS MOMENTS

Joy

Joy is the feeling of grinning inside.
MELBA COLGROVE

*Satisfy us in the morning with your unfailing love, that we may
sing for joy and be glad all our days.*
PSALM 90:14

Most mornings, our bed resembles the set of a coffee commercial. In the wee hours, Peyton scampers to our room and crawls in bed with us. Then Morgan stirs and joins us. We snuggle in a cozy bundle. It is picture perfect. You can almost smell the coffee brewing, or so it would seem. While our mornings may be about togetherness, they are definitely not about sleep.

When Peyton climbs into bed, she crawls over her dad like a mountaineer climbing Everest. Half asleep, she flops down between us, arms outstretched. Pete and I scoot aside, making way for our not-so-little bed hog. Just as I get comfortable, achieving perfect under-the-cover coziness, she starts to kick, frantically pushing off the comforter as she rides an imaginary unicycle at world record pace. Pete and I pull the covers up; she kicks them off again.

When Morgan joins us, she is always accompanied by a crew of friends and sometimes our dog Trapper. She haphazardly throws her stuffed pals up first, pulling any remaining covers off as she shimmies up the side of the mattress. Once Morgan is settled,

Peyton starts to flip like a fish on a boat deck, arms and legs flailing once more. Pete, Morgan and I all scooch to the edges of the bed to avoid the manic octopus—and while Morgan falls back to sleep, Pete and I cannot. By now we are wide awake. Though we love togetherness and snuggling with our kids, our bed has become an epicenter of bedlam.

"I guess I'll go make us some joe," Pete says. (This is the closest we ever get to the smooth coffee commercial.)

I get up, pull Peyton to Pete's side, prop pillows around Morgan and follow my husband to the kitchen.

"Can you imagine if we had more kids?" he asks, handing me a cup of java.

"No," I say with a laugh. "Do they make a mattress that big?"

"It wouldn't fit in our bedroom!" he says, laughing.

As I head to the shower, I peek at the sweet, sleeping souls who have kidnapped our place of peaceful repose. This is our daily routine, and I would not change a thing. Though we could take measures to reclaim our sleeping quarters, we do not. We savor this time and start each day with a joyful dose of kid-wiggling craziness. Waking up this way may be unorthodox, but it sure beats a standard alarm clock.

Savoring Life

Though I experience joy apart from my girls, the delight they give is like having a strawberry dipped in Godiva chocolate: a sweet blessing! Children are high-energy guides from Heavenly Tours, Inc. My daughters are precious gifts from God; being around them helps me tune into bliss, giving me perspective and eyes to see the treasure in moments I normally would skim over like a high schooler with CliffsNotes. My girls are a reminder that all true joy comes from God.

Understanding God as the source, joy becomes water pouring over a dam that has reached capacity, happiness overflowing into everything. For me, some of these moments include Peyton's and Morgan's sweet voices filling our home; running in the ocean, laughing and splashing in the waves; picking berries still warm from the sun and getting purple fingers and sticky smiles; snuggled up together reading books during a snowstorm; tearing open an unexpected package from Grandma with goodies for all. You may have a similar list of joy moments, for surely such moments jump at us just waiting to be caught and savored. God is the well-spring from which the waters of contented thankfulness flow. God gives us this joy in good times, of course, but also in difficult circumstances that work to dull our awareness of joy.

> *"I hope you find joy in the great things in life—but also in the little things. A flower, a song, a butterfly on your hand."* —ELLEN LEVINE

When Peyton was hospitalized for a brain tumor, I stayed with her the entire month. (No job stress, no teachers, no homework and no email. When does *that* ever happen?) Despite the difficulties of our situation, God was with us and blessed our time together. Sipping hot chocolate and watching videos together from her hospital bed reminded me to be joyful for all types of blessings. With God as my source, joy came from the inside, transcending the circumstances, keeping me afloat.

God's Natural Sweetness

Helen Keller once said, "Joy is the holy fire that keeps our purpose warm and intelligence aglow." I believe the "holy fire" she is describing is an understanding of the eternal God. Understanding our true connection to God in redemption and reconciliation to Him through Christ is the essence of true joy. You see, joy isn't a coincidence; it is a spiritual reality. When we understand our true connection to God, we connect with all that He is and all that we are in Him. A relationship with God through Christ gives us meaning in every moment and joy in the journey. Many of us spend our whole life searching for relationships and things to give us that feeling—from shopping to food to drugs and more, but all the substitutes only give a temporary feeling of elation; true joy is rooted in God—the only source of joy.

A Cup of Joy

With the indwelling of God's presence in our life through the Holy Spirit, we can tap into an eternal sense of wellbeing every moment of every day. Like a massive floodlight shining into every facet of our life, the wonderful moments get brighter—and the deep, lonely places are not so dark and desolate, because God's heavenly illumination brings joy into every situation. Even in moments of despair, His light is there, steady and shining. "For the joy of the LORD is your strength" (Nehemiah 8:10).

"May the God of hope fill you with all joy and peace as you trust in Him, so that you may overflow with hope by the power of the Holy Spirit." —ROMANS 15:13

Joy is truly a gift. Grasp it. Seek Jesus and savor the sweetness of joy like a child with a lollipop. Savor laughter, hugs, watching your children sleep, clean plates at dinnertime, a soft chair, an understanding smile, a cup of coffee, a scoop of ice cream, a word of thanks. Simple and big moments of joy are available like a cornucopia at Thanksgiving, overflowing and precious, from God alone.

Questions to STIR

1. Think of moments with your children during a typical day. Do these times bring you joy? How can you savor them more?

2. Think of a recent challenge or mountain you had to climb in your life. Did you look for joy in the journey? How can you thank Jesus for joy, despite different circumstances?

3. Look up "joy" in a concordance or reference Bible. Read several of the verses and try to find application in your recent experience.

Soul Sip Solutions

1. Go to one of your favorite places and look at it with "new" eyes. Look carefully for all the small delights in God's creation that bring you joy. Example: a local botanical garden, a sandy beach, a park.

2. Think of something that brought you joy as a child. Do it again— with your own child (children). Savor each moment.

3. Over the course of the next week, make note of all the things that bring you joy. Give thanks to God for His consistent blessing.

Reflection and Challenge

How can you proclaim your joy to God? Journal your thoughts.

_____

_____

_____

_____

_____

_____

_____

_____

_____

_____

_____

_____

_____

_____

_____

_____

_____

_____

24

HEAVENLY BREW

Hope

Learn from yesterday, live for today, hope for tomorrow.
ALBERT EINSTEIN

Hope deferred makes the heart sick, but a longing fulfilled is a tree of life.
PROVERBS 13:12

I did not want to get out of bed. I could tell from the gray light filtering in through the windows that the day was overcast—and since it was January, assuredly cold. It had been frigid and overcast for more than a week and I, like a solar-powered grid, was ready for a change. Actually, I was ready for more than just a little bit of sunshine: I was ready for some life change.

I sighed, rolled over and snuggled into the reassurance of the blankets. Pete's side of the bed was empty; he was likely on his second cup of coffee, down working in his office. The girls, on winter break, were still asleep. The house was quiet. My mind, on the other hand, was not. Templeton (see chapter 2), my treadmill rat, raced around, chewing on thoughts and spitting them out, littering my psyche with discouragement and garbage. Finances were tight and my writing career seemed stuck; rejection slips had been pouring in and I, like a down pillow run over by a truck, felt flat and empty.

"Hey, you," my husband's voice ended Templeton's party. "Time to get up. Brought you some coffee." He set the cup on the nightstand and sat down next to me on the bed. "What's up with you, huh? You don't seem your normal, cheery self."

"Oh, I dunno," I said. "I guess I'm just discouraged. I feel like my writing is never going to take off. It's a bunch of stuff, I guess."

"Well," said my husband, smiling, "maybe today will be your day. Maybe someone will say yes to your book. Don't let a few nos get you down. You're stronger than that."

"Oh, I guess you're right," I said, grumbling, encouraged by my personal cheerleader. I knew things would get better and I had no reason to sulk. I sat up and took a sip of coffee. Just then, the rest of the pep squad bounded into the room.

"Mommy! Mommy! What are we going to do today? Can we go to the movies? Make cookies? Go to the park? Get up! Let's go! Let's go!"

Just then, the sun broke through the clouds.

"An acre of coffee trees can produce up to 10,000 pounds of coffee cherries." —GOURMETCOFFEECLUB.COM[1]

An Antidote for Discouragement

What gets you out of bed in the morning? What draws you out from the sheets in anticipation of each new day? What lights your fire? What do you hope for?

Hope. Hope is the feeling of anticipation when you are sitting in a movie theater—popcorn in hand—waiting for the show to begin. It is two blue lines on a positive pregnancy test. Hope looks like the gummy smile of a new baby; sounds like the blades of a rescue helicopter when you are lost at sea; and feels like a child, face to the sky, tongue outstretched, waiting to catch a snowflake.

According to Webster's dictionary, hope is defined as "the feeling that what is wanted can be had or that events will turn out for the best."[2] A good definition, but hope has an even greater scope than this definition implies. It is bigger than wanting stuff or a particular outcome: It is a heavenly expectation of an abundant life when our faith is placed in God. Hope looks forward to the future, having trust and confidence in God's omnipotence. Hope is the essence of possibility—because God is the essence of possibility—for "all things are possible with God" (Mark 10:27).

It is so easy to get bogged down in disappointments, failures and loss. The morning I did not want to get out of bed, I wasn't seeing all that God has for me, that day or in the future. My husband's cheerful comments (and the piping-hot coffee) helped wake me up to the reality that *there is always hope*. Charles L. Allen once said, "When you say a person or situation is hopeless, you are slamming a door in the face of God." Ouch. It is easy to focus on the doors being slammed (rejection, illness, fatigue, failures) and not see things from God's perspective. He never leaves us. George Wienberg once stated, "Hope never abandons you; you abandon it." We place our hope in God, knowing He is eternal, and He is faithful (see 2 Thessalonians 3:3).

Good Things in Store

A few years ago, I wanted to purchase a hope chest for each of my girls. I thought a cedar chest would be a great place to collect keepsake items like preschool art, report cards and baby shoes. While researching where to buy such a chest, I came across the origin of the term. A "hope chest," also sometimes called a "glory box," was designed to be a chest in which a young girl collected clothes, bed linens, towels, dishes and such in anticipation of marriage.

The hope chest concept got me thinking: Nothing will happen unless we take action to prepare for what we envision and hope for in life: The essence of hope is working together with God to make our dreams a reality. When our hope is in God, we honor Him with our belief, assured of His provision—not knowing when or how He's going to provide—only that He will.

"Those who hope in the LORD will renew their strength. They will soar on wings like eagles; they will run and not grow weary, they will walk and not be faint." —ISAIAH 40:31

If you have hope, it is not just a happy accident. God gives you hope. Hope entails trust, confidence and obedience. It means you are looking to God, seeking His will, asking Him to show up and then doing all you can to meet Him there.

A Cup of Hope

Hope is more than wishful thinking. Hope is anticipation of a life filled with purpose and blessing. No matter how dark our days may seem (or how cozy our sheets), we all have a reason to get out of bed in the morning: We have a true "glory box" of hope in God. God says in Jeremiah 29:11, "For I know the plans I have for you . . . plans to prosper you and not to harm you, plans to give you hope and a future." God has great things in store for us, and hope is fulfilled when we meet Him with obedience, faithfulness and patience. What we hope for does not always come in the way (or time frame) we would like. Be patient. In Romans 12:12, Paul reminds us to be "joyful in hope, patient in affliction, and faithful in prayer." Accept God's cup of hope and watch the sun rise on your life.

Questions to STIR

1. What gets you out of bed in the morning? What gives you hope with each new day?

2. Are you guilty of abandoning hope—even in any teeny-weeny area of your life? How can you trust God more and take action toward the glorious life He has for you?

3. Read Isaiah 40:31. What does it mean to put your hope in the Lord? Think of the power in the promise of this verse. How does this give you hope?

Soul Sip Solutions

1. Talk with your children about hope. What does it mean to them? Tell them what it means to you.

2. What do you hope for? Write a list. Pray and give the list to God.

3. Take one action step on each of the items on your list from Soul Sip #2. For example, if you hope to win a chili cook-off,

maybe it's time to cook up a pot and hone your recipe. If your hope is to lose a few pounds, go for a walk.

Reflection and Challenge

I like to think that my husband is a mind reader when I "hope" he will take out the trash, send me flowers or tell me I look beautiful. Next time you are tempted to hope that your husband (or anyone) will read your mind, take action and help him know what you need or like. Record the result.

_____

_____

_____

_____

_____

_____

_____

_____

_____

_____

_____

_____

_____

_____

_____

_____

_____

_____

_____

_____

25

THIS CAME
FROM A BEAN?

Faith

*Faith is deliberate confidence in the character of God whose
ways you may not understand at the time.*
OSWALD CHAMBERS

*And without faith it is impossible to please God, because
anyone who comes to him must believe that he exists and that
he rewards those who earnestly seek him.*
HEBREWS 11:6

When it comes to coffee, I've got lots of faith. I've got faith that the drink will be what I ordered; faith that the caffeine will be the pick-me-up I am looking for; faith that I'll have enough cash for my tasty indulgence; and faith that I'll make it to work on time despite the detour to Starbucks on an already tight schedule. I can't recount how many times I have stopped to get coffee five minutes before a morning meeting, only to end up tardy. On some level, I know the timing will not work out, but I am unable to envision a two-hour meeting without a latte to keep me awake.

I am one block away. If there's no line, I can park, grab my coffee and be back in three minutes. Then zip across the street and be right on time.

This is never the case. One of two scenarios usually happens:

Scenario One: The waiting line is six deep. I hope everyone ahead of me will order drip coffee and the line will move quickly. This doesn't happen, so I abandon all coffee hope, rush out the door, zip across the street, hit a red light, wait what seems an eternity and am still late . . . and caffeine-free.

Scenario Two: A lady enters the coffee shop with me, but there is no line. Being the thoughtful woman I am, I hold the door for her. "Thank you," she says and proceeds to the counter. I scan the menu in anticipation of my morning indulgence, certain to be on time.

"With the exception of Hawaii and Puerto Rico,
no coffee is grown in the United States or its territories."

—GOURMETCOFFEECLUB.COM[1]

"Okay, I have a list for you," she tells the barista. "I need a large latte, two small mochas, an Americana, an orange slush, and two regular coffees with room for cream."

Is she kidding? She has coffee orders for her whole office! I am so close; I cannot walk away. I glance at my watch every fifteen seconds, trying to will time to stop. It doesn't. I finally get my coffee, rush to the car, slosh it on the console, hit the red light, and again I'm late—and also too embarrassed to walk in with coffee, the clear cause of my delay. So I pitch what's left.

Faith in Daily Life

We all put our faith in something. We have faith in our parents, our boss, our bank, our education, our leaders, our friends, our marriage vows. We put faith in our refrigerator, our under-eye concealer, our bras, our coffee. I put my faith in the local barista, confident she will deliver the drink I've asked for; I don't stand and watch to make sure she puts in nonfat milk or the right amount of espresso. I don't pop the lid to get a look before I drink; when my order is up, I just grab and sip. That's faith: trusting in someone or something, assured that the outcome will be good.

Faith is so basic, really. Yet, when it comes to professing faith in God, well, it creates quite a hullabaloo; it is one of those things that gets people all stirred up with their britches in a bundle. Why?

Faith seems easy in day-to-day stuff—like trusting the chair will hold when we sit down—but when it comes to faith in the eternal, unseen God, well, that's a bit scarier.

But the only way to come to God is through faith; there is no other way. Faith is "being sure of what we hope for and certain of what we do not see" (Hebrews 11:1). Faith is trusting though we don't yet understand. We don't get a deposit receipt to see where our investment has gone; it is an act of our will—a step into the unknown—with a payoff bigger than our finite minds can comprehend. Where do we get the courage to take this step of faith? We get it from God; it's a mysterious tug at our heartstrings, a silent beckoning we can't rationally explain.

> "Now faith is being sure of what we hope for and certain of what we do not see." —HEBREWS 11:1

In a recent conversation with a friend, my husband encountered lots of hotbed issues in their discussion. "I don't have all the answers," my husband said. "All I can tell you is that I believe in God and know that when I am walking with Jesus, my life is a whole lot better. I know in my heart that He is real, even though I can't physically see Him, because I've felt His power in my life."

The Faith Relationship

When we experience God's power, it is easier to live by faith in other areas. We can embrace possibilities that don't seem safe or, at times, even rational to the average person. God often calls people to act in faith—trusting Him, stepping into the unknown. I have friends with small children who have been called from comfortable suburban lives to work in foreign countries as missionaries. I know others who have sold everything to go into ministry work. God asks us to trust Him, no matter the risk, and He rewards our willingness to step out in faith.

Faith is not a matter of what we trust but in whom we trust. Hebrews 12:2 states, "Let us fix our eyes on Jesus, the author and perfecter of our faith." Faith grows in our life when we keep our eyes on God. "By faith we understand that the universe was formed at God's command" (Hebrews 11:3). The author of Hebrews gives us examples of many individuals who by faith pleased God. And where did their faith come from? From God Himself. When we come to God, believing, the more we grow in our relationship with Him, the stronger our faith grows.

A Cup of Faith

When I think about the mighty power of God, I am ashamed at my general lack of faith. God has *every detail of my life*—down to the electric bill, the commute and the water I drink—and as such, I should trust Him with everything.

Matthew 15:21-28 tells the story of a woman whose daughter was possessed by demons, and she sought Jesus to heal her child. She humbled herself and persisted until God healed her daughter, saying, "Woman, you have great faith! Your request is granted" (Matthew 15:28).

Luke 8 tells a similar story of a woman who had been bleeding for 12 years. No one could heal her, so when Jesus passed, she reached out from the crowd to grab His cloak (a very brazen move in her time). When Jesus asked who had touched Him, she came forward and explained why she had done it, seeking His healing power. Jesus told her, "Daughter, your faith has healed you. Go in peace" (Luke 8:48).

Although the Bible is jam-packed with stories of faith, these two women come to mind as examples of persistent seeking and confidence in God. What would things be like for us if we had such radical faith in God? How might our lives be different?

We so easily put our faith in things that eventually fail: the stock market, world leaders, our Spanx underwear . . . but God never fails. He never has and never will. When we have confidence and trust in God, He grows us—and our faith—like a sunflower in the garden of life, getting bigger and more vibrant as it rises toward its Source. A sunflower does not have eyes; it just feels the light and moves toward it. So it is with faith. We don't have to "see" it. "We live by faith, not by sight" (2 Corinthians 5:7).

Carved in the front of an ancient mantel in the Hind's Head Hotel in Bray, England, there is this saying: "Fear knocked at the door. Faith answered. No one was there." Perhaps the "ancients" won't mind me putting a spin on their saying: Fear knocked at the door. Faith answered and was rewarded. For God was there.

Questions to STIR

1. What things do you put your faith in on a daily basis? Why might it sometimes seem easier to trust a stranger than God?

2. Reread Hebrews 11:6. How can you "earnestly seek" God? How can you walk more in faith? If you have questions about your faith, what steps can you take to seek answers?

3. Does putting complete trust in God scare you? Why/why not?

Soul Sip Solutions

1. Think of a dream or a goal you have sidelined because it felt impossible. If you still feel strongly about it, how might you have more faith to try again?

2. Think of three areas of your life in which you could have more faith. Pray and surrender these to God. Ask Him to grow your faith.

3. No matter where you are in your spiritual journey, ask God to grow your faith. Persistently seek Him this week.

Reflection and Challenge

Faith is not a set of rules to live by. Faith is simply putting your hope and trust in God. What misconceptions might you have about faith? How can you put more faith in Jesus? Record your thoughts.

_____

_____

_____

_____

_____

_____

COFFEE BREAK
WITH BETH

Dear Moms,

Are you struggling with doubt in your life? I've been where you are—doubting. I know what it's like to be a "me-of-little-faith" woman. Circumstances knocked me off my feet and knocked my faith off its foundations too.

I was disappointed in God. I was disappointed in myself. I felt like God let me down when my prayers went unanswered—or weren't answered the way I'd hoped. I felt like I let God down when I didn't joyfully persevere through the tough times. Neither of us had been faithful to each other—or so it seemed.

Doubt is a lonely place. Life is still hard—and I couldn't turn to the God of all comfort. Life has its moments of joy too—and yet, who do you praise when you and God aren't speaking to one another?

I never doubted God's existence. I just doubted His faithfulness. Yet, even in the midst of my doubt, I missed God. I found myself coming near to God again, thinking, "Maybe He'll forgive me for not trusting Him." I felt like the wretched prodigal daughter, returning home in all my dirt. I didn't deserve to be forgiven.

The minute I turned back to God and said, "I'm sorry," He pulled me close to His heart and said, "I've been waiting for you." Romans 8:38-39 says that nothing can separate me from God's love—not even my lack of faith. I let our relationship get strained for a while—for too long. But God never stopped loving me, never stopped extending His grace. I just refused to see it.

Doubt will come in every believer's life. When it does, we have a choice: Allow doubt to drive us away from God or closer to Him. Don't deny it if you're a "she-of-little-faith." God knows it—and He loves you just as you are, doubts and all.

Beth Vogt

2 6

WITH CREAM AND SUGAR

Love and Kindness

The little unremembered acts of kindness and love are the best parts of a person's life.
WILLIAM WORDSWORTH

Love is patient, love is kind.
1 CORINTHIANS 13:4

It was one of those mornings. You know the type. My sea of sleep had been filled with whitecap waves that tossed me about the bed like the *SS Minnow*, and I awoke a shipwreck. I was grouchy and exhausted, hoping a cup of coffee would give me the fuel to navigate back to friendly waters.

When I arrived at work, I grabbed my cup and went straight to the kitchen. There, crowded around the coffee pot like a convention from *Loveboat*, were several of my all-too-perky coworkers.

"So, how was your vacation?" one of the women asked Sue, just back from a trip.

"It was great. I ate a lot, napped by the pool and even read two books! I LOVED it!"

"What books did you read?" asked another coworker.

"*The Secret Life of Bees* . . . and um . . . another one called *Breathe*."

"I LOVED *The Secret Life of Bees*!" exclaimed Jena. "It's such a great read."

"I LOVED it too," agreed Sue. "It made me cry at the end."

Just as the coffee was done, Luann rushed into the office, paper cup in hand. "Oh my gosh," she blurted, "you guys have to try this new coffee! It is so tasty. I LOVE it!"

She offered her drink to the few who wanted a taste.

"No, thanks," said Sue. "I'll pass."

"Luanne, I LOVE your shoes," Jena said with a catty purr.

"Thanks, I got them yesterday."

Just then the coffee maker beeped, signaling it was time to fill our cups and get to work. As I walked to my office, I couldn't help notice this morning's dialogue had been a regular LOVE-fest, but the superficial love-ins were annoying. I didn't have the energy—especially on this morning. I closed my office door; it was quiet and still. *Now this*, I thought, *I LOVE!*

The Mechanism for Love

Is it just me, or has the term "love" become a bit overused? It's like a toddler's watered-down apple juice—not as sweet as the undiluted original. These days, we say "love" when referring to a stylish pair of jeans, a tasty new recipe or most anything we have a fleeting affection for. That's not really love, but a generic blanket covering a lazy vocabulary.

"And let us consider how we may spur one another on toward love and good deeds. Let us not give up meeting together, as some are in the habit of doing, but let us encourage one another."

—Hebrews 10:24-25

I have to admit, I'm rarely touched and usually skeptical when it comes to random proclamations of love; a group email blast affectionately signed "Luv U!" hardly strums my heartstrings. In fact, the cynic in me wonders if the sender really knows what love is.

If we are fortunate, the people who truly love us will tell us on a regular basis and demonstrate their love through kindness. Like the vacuum tube that transports the canister of cash to the teller at the drive-thru bank, kindness is a delivery system for the riches of love.

God describes the many characteristics of love in 1 Corinthians 13. No doubt love encompasses much, but kindness is the attribute that actually helps others perceive they are cared for: a hand extended, a gentle word, a smile when needed most. Those who love you are the ones who will—at five in the morning—go out in the middle of a blizzard to rescue you when your car is stuck in a snow embankment 20 miles away. Love is a father telling his daughter, "I am so proud of you!" or "You are lovely!" Love is your husband putting a single rose on your pillow while you nap. Love is a million kind acts performed without any expectation of reciprocation. Love is kindness freely bestowed; kindness is love freely bestowed.

Not-So-Random Acts of Kindness

Just over a year ago, my husband's company closed its doors. Though our family was able to live off savings until he was established with a new company, we cut back on all superfluous spending, watching every penny.

My birthday came along a few months into his joblessness—and though I had been hoping for some funky new red glasses, we really didn't have the "extra" money to spend. I was sick with a cold the whole week and feeling crummy. Then our daughter Peyton had some health tests that did not have the reassuring results I'd been praying for.

Quite honestly, I was stressed about our finances, physically and mentally fatigued and fearful about our daughter's long-term health. I'd been dragged into discouragement's dungeon and the darkness was closing in quickly. I collapsed on the living room floor and cried out to God. (It's a good thing God knows me so well, because anyone other than He would not have been able to understand me through the sobs and snot.) I asked God to hear me, to heal Peyton, to help us. I asked Him for encouragement.

Just then I had an immediate, specific feeling that I should buy Peyton some balloons and take them to her school. *Show her you love her* was what I felt God telling me to do. So I jumped in my car and drove to the store.

The selection of Mylar balloons seemed average—of course, just my luck. I wanted to find something special, but all they had were plain round "Happy Birthday" and "Get Well" varieties. Then the clerk pulled out a few new packages—and showed me some big butterfly styles. They were gorgeous and multicolored, just what I was looking for.

"Which one do you want?" she asked.

"I'll take both," I said, knowing the purchase might not be within our budget.

On a small card, I wrote, "Peyton, I am so proud of you. You are a great big sister, and you make me smile every day. Love, Mom."

When I walked into the school, the ladies at the front desk asked, "Ohhh, is it her birthday?"

"No," I said. "I just want to make her feel special."

"How sweet," they said. "We'll deliver them to her classroom."

"Thanks," I said, handing over the big butterflies. I was starting to feel better; taking action to show my daughter love had improved my own spirits.

Right before I got home, I stopped to get the mail. Atop the stack of catalogs and bills was a small letter for me. I tore it open and there on the front of the card were two multicolored butterflies. I gasped. It was a note from a friend at church, which read:

"I remember being a young mom on a tight budget. Here is a little something for you. Treat yourself to something special." Enclosed was a check—with the exact dollar amount I needed for the red glasses.

☕ *"Let love and faithfulness never leave you; bind them around your neck, write them on the tablet of your heart."* —Proverbs 3:3

Once again, I collapsed in tears, needing windshield wipers for my eyes to navigate home. I could barely drive. What touched me so deeply was not the money, but the kindness of another in my time of need. My friend didn't know about Peyton's tests or that I'd been sick. She just acted out of love. God's timing was perfect. I cried happy tears for what seemed like days.

Now, skeptics might think the butterflies were a coincidence, but I know better. The butterflies were a clear sign to me that God was in every detail. What might have seemed random acts of kindness were not so random at all. The events were woven together by God to give me the quilt of encouragement I'd asked for in prayer.

A Cup of Love and Kindness

John Watson once said, "Be kind—everyone you meet is fighting a hard battle." (Sigh.) It's a tough world. Everyone needs encouragement; everyone needs love. Yet to some degree, love as we know it today has become a generic currency unable to give us the heart payoff we so desperately seek.

True kindness, shown through simple acts with big meaning, is one way we can demonstrate real love. When it comes right down to it, love is a choice, an action. Love shown through kindness is not defined by deservedness; it is found in God's example of unconditional love. The fuel that runs the kindness engine is God's love in the heart of the person doing the loving.

We learn to love by being loved. We learn to be kind by receiving kindness. This love is from God alone—no matter what we've done or how horrible we feel, He loves us (see 1 John 4:19). When our hearts are filled with God's love—and yielded to Him—He enables us to share that which we have received. Lovingkindness is a heavenly pay-it-forward in which we may never see the results of our actions but are assured they will be used by God for good—to touch lives—and occasionally show us the world through rose-colored glasses.

Questions to STIR

1. How do the people you love know you really care? Do you show them or just tell them? Do your actions contradict your words?

2. What do you consider the most important qualities in love? When someone loves you, where does kindness fall on the list?

3. Look to the example of Jesus (see Ephesians 4:32). How might you practically show others you love them?

Soul Sip Solutions

1. How is being "kind" different from being "nice"? Is someone who is nice always kind?

2. Think of a time someone showed you they loved and cared for you through a simple action. How did it make you feel?

3. How might you act in lovingkindness toward someone this week?

Reflection and Challenge

No matter how loving we are, we can all learn to love others more. What are some ways you can show love to others more? Pray and ask God to continue to grow your heart in love and kindness.

_____

_____

_____

_____

_____

_____

_____

_____

_____

_____

_____

_____

2 7

A DOUBLE ESPRESSO

Strength

*Strength is the ability to break a chocolate bar into four pieces with your
bare hands—and then just eat one of those pieces.*
JUDITH VIORST

*The LORD is my strength and my shield; my heart trusts in him,
and I am helped.*
PSALM 28:7

What is strength and where does it come from? Do we get strength
at the gym—building and toning our muscles with exercises and
resistance training? Do we get it from eating the right foods—like
Popeye and his can of spinach? Or do we get strength from coffee—
downing a triple-shot espresso to propel us through the day?

I was curious what my friends thought about strength—so I
asked.

What Is Strength?

"Strength is gritting your teeth in spite of all that happens, and
pressing through even when you think you can't." —Lesley B.

"[Strength is] when you don't quit." —Monica D.

"Strength is knowing that tomorrow is another day, and I can get
through today." —Heather P.

"[Strength is being] unshakeable. That doesn't mean you don't get
bent, but that you're still intact." —Nancy V.

"Strength is having big pipes [muscles]." —Morgan, age 4

"Strength . . . is the motivation to get up out of a soft, warm bed . . . when you are physically exhausted, because your baby is sick, needs to be fed, or has a bad dream. Strength is something God gives me when I need to keep going." —Tammy J.

"[Strength is] being brave." —Peyton, age 9

"Strength is having hope and seeing the good . . . at your lowest point." —Erika W.

"Strength is going the extra distance when you feel like you can't take another step. Strength is supporting someone who needs you, even when you need someone to support you!" —Ashley G.

Where Do You Get Your Strength?

"I get my strength from God. Period." —Susan H.

"When I think of being strong, I think of depending on God. And that seems an oxymoron because of the 'dependence' . . . but I get my strength from God." —Laurie C.

"At my age, I couldn't even make it through the day without asking God for strength at the beginning of each morning!" —Carol K.

"I do my devotional at 4:30 every morning, before Starbucks even opens. And I am faithful at Starbucks—they know my name and my drink. But . . . God is my strength." —Debbie B.

When I Am Weak . . .

We all have different definitions of strength. Overall, strength is the power that enables us to prevail in life's challenges. Whether it is a mile-long hill on a morning jog, some type of loss, or a challenge we must conquer like the pop-ups on a video game, life's road always has obstacles. Strength determines if we will claim the prize like the winners on the *Amazing Race* or collapse and falter mid-journey.

There are many types of strength: physical, mental and spiritual. Each contributes to the other—working synergistically to arm us for life's battles.

Physical prowess is an important component of being strong. Our body is God's temple, and fitness honors Him. When our bodies and hearts are strong, we may not be able to bend steel like Superman or lift cars like Mr. Incredible, but we can lift grocery bags and play with our children without wearing down. When physically strong, we have more endurance for all types of work—and will be ready to help someone when needed—*Mom to the rescue!*

☕ *God's strength is available if we just acknowledge and accept it.*

Mental strength is the discipline of resolve and strength of character. Resolve is the will to follow things through to the end, to be determined, focused, purposeful and undeterred. Strength of resolve is following through when you feel physically wiped out like a runner in the last mile of a marathon. Resolve is persisting through obstacles. Resolve is relying on God, knowing that He will give us the strength to get through anything. Thomas Merton once said, "Perhaps I am stronger than I think." In fact, *we all are stronger than we think*. God is a limitless source of strength. That knowledge gives us resolve. Strength of character becomes evident when we exercise the moral fortitude in doing the right thing, in making right choices.

Spiritual strength is knowing that we can do anything with God on our side (see Philippians 4:13). When we are filled with the Fruit of the Spirit (see Galatians 5:22-23), we have the qualities of God working in and through us. We can act with goodness, love and compassion. We can be strong for others in addition to ourselves. Spiritual power is available to us through faith alone; no gym membership required.

God's Perfect Strength

We need only trust in God and we are helped. It may be hard to remember this in the midst of a trial, but God's strength is available if we just acknowledge and accept it. My friend Holly, a mother of two, shares her story:

"I really struggled when Lauren, my second daughter, was born; I lost all my free time. With Ashley . . . I had downtime when she was sleeping. But both daughters took up so much of my time, I couldn't do the things I wanted to do. I know it sounds selfish, but I was actually upset when I was unable to sit, uninterrupted, to watch my favorite television show.

"One night when Lauren was two months old, and not sleeping well, I was so tired and frustrated, I harshly asked her, 'What's the matter with you?!' I quickly realized how stupid my question was. My [infant] daughter didn't know what was wrong and couldn't control herself. Why was I trying to reason with her?

"It was then I started praying relentlessly for God to change me. I asked Him to change the way I thought about *my* time. I started to thank God every time I had to get up at night or interrupt what I was doing to care for my daughters. I thanked Him for giving me children. I prayed for His strength to get me through the days when I had little sleep. So far, God has completely changed my point of view, transforming my 'burden' into a true blessing.

    "The Sovereign Lord is my strength." —HABAKKUK 3:19

"Strength means I can get through anything. Not that everything in life will go smoothly or that I'll make it through flawlessly, but I know God will get me through and I *will* make it. I know 100 percent that my strength comes from God."

A Cup of Strength

The need for strength is a reality for today's busy mom. I need it. You need it. And guess what? God has it for us. Life is lived on a battlefield; we all have wars to fight. This is not a clever analogy; it is the truth. The enemy is real. Fight for the fullness of life God has for you and your family. Know that God fights for you (see Joshua 23:10). Be strong. Arm yourself by putting your trust in the Lord.

"The Lord is my strength and my shield; my heart trusts in Him, and I am helped" (Psalm 28:7).

Ephesians 6:10-18 tells us to arm ourselves for life's battles with God's armor: "Be strong in the Lord and in his mighty power. Put on the full armor of God so that . . . you may be able to stand your ground . . . with the belt of truth buckled around your waist, with the breastplate of righteousness in place, and with your feet fitted with the readiness that comes from the gospel of peace. In addition to this, take up the shield of faith . . . the helmet of salvation and the sword of the Spirit, which is the word of God. And pray in the Spirit . . . be alert and always keep on praying."

After reading this passage, can't you just feel God's strength?

Questions to STIR

1. What is your personal definition of strength? Where do you turn for strength in times of need?

2. Are you physically, mentally and spiritually strong? What areas do you need to focus on? How can you gain strength in each of these areas?

3. Read Mark 12:30. What would it look like to love God with all your strength? What kind of strength would that give you in return? How would this affect the strength and example you give to your children?

Soul Sip Solutions

1. If you, like me, have strong fingers and a "computer butt," maybe you need some strength training. Make it a priority to fit in one workout this week.

2. Next time you encounter a battle, arm yourself with God's armor. Pray out loud (from Ephesians 6:10-18) and ask God to cloak you in His armor.

3. Read 1 Chronicles 16:11. How can you seek His face always?

Reflection and Challenge

Do 10 pushups and read one Proverb every day this week. Feel yourself becoming stronger. Write down some of your thoughts about what you learned from the experience.

_____
_____
_____
_____
_____
_____
_____
_____
_____
_____
_____
_____
_____
_____
_____
_____
_____
_____
_____
_____
_____
_____

28

SECURITY SMOOTHIE

Peace

It isn't enough to talk about peace. One must believe in it. And it isn't enough to believe in it. One must work at it.
ELEANOR ROOSEVELT

We have peace with God through our Lord Jesus Christ.
ROMANS 5:1

"Mommy! Mommy! I had an accident!" my potty-training toddler urgently announced, interrupting my morning coffee and catapulting me toward the day—full sprint.

I clean up the piddle puddle, then get dressed, pulling on a new white Banana Republic T-shirt and a favorite pair of pink plaid shorts. I corral and feed the kids, then direct them toward the car like a rancher prodding her herd. As we pull out of the driveway, I realize I don't have a cup-o-java. I run back in, fill a thermos mug, then like Flash Gordon, I'm back in the car, zipping down the mommy-chaos highway.

I drop daughter number one at day camp and head to swimming lessons with daughter number two. I carry her in one arm, pool bag slung over my shoulder, coffee in the other hand. Once we get poolside, however, I need both hands to help my little one shimmy into her swim diaper and suit. So I tuck my coffee cup into the side pocket of the bag and bend over to assist.

As I pull the tight blue diaper up over her little sausage legs, I feel a warm sensation on my back. It's like liquid sunshine spreading . . . like . . . like . . . COFFEE! It takes little more than an instant for me to realize my error, but by then it is too late. I have a basketball-size coffee stain covering the middle of my back—framed by the bright white of my never-yet-worn, brand-new shirt.

I dive into a lounge chair, concealing my clumsy gaffe for the 30 minutes my daughter swims. But too soon I'm at the edge of the pool, offering a towel and a smile for my drenched daughter. I put a towel over my own shoulders and pull my soggy little swimmer to my chest, wrapping her in a mom-hug embrace. Of course, now the front of my shirt is wet too—but my daughter provides a protective shield and the towel hides my coffee faux pas. At world-record pace, we dash to the car, successfully avoiding the curious glances of my mommy peers, and plow home.

"*Detached from Christ, inner peace is a kind of spiritual marshmallow, full of softness and sweetness but without much actual substance.*" —Nicky Gumbel, *Questions of Life*[1]

On the drive home, the radio plays a song about being filled with peace. *Peace? What peace?* I wonder. I couldn't quite tap in. Rush, mess, spills and franticness typify my life—not peace and serenity. Where was the disconnect? What was I missing—besides a clean, dry T-shirt?

Tranquility in Turmoil

You probably can relate to the Mom Rush. Some days, peace only comes for me when I've demanded too much of myself and I blow a circuit. This is not the ideal path. Peace is not sitting on the living room couch in a catatonic state, unable to function because every neuron in your body is zapped. Peace is an inner tranquility found *amid* the rush and routine; it is a heavenly calm that carries us through the coffee spills, late-night homework, last-minute deadlines, carpooling, and all the rest.

We tap into this calm when we make God the *first* priority of our day and in our life. Admittedly, when mornings start with screaming toddlers, it can be hard to find quiet time. Yet, a morning habit of time with Jesus will give us the sustenance we need for the day ahead despite the surprise ketchup squirts when life puts "the squeeze" on us.

Making our spiritual life a priority is the best thing we can do for ourselves and for those we love; it is the launching point for lasting peace. Peace comes when we seek the Lord, arranging (and rearranging) priorities, putting God first.

Peace means creating some breathing room. Not long ago, a wise friend told me, "I am praying for you to have healthy margin in your life." Margin? At first, I didn't know what she meant. Then I thought about it. A margin is a border, a perimeter, a boundary. It is the area of space we give ourselves around "life." Richard Swenson, in his book *Margin,* calls it "the gap between rest and exhaustion, the space between breathing freely and suffocating."[2] For me, that's usually not much room. Margins give us the time and the space to downshift, pray and refocus. If you schedule appointments five minutes apart throughout the day and allow no time for rest stops or bathroom breaks, you lack margin.

Building a healthy margin is easier said than done. It requires setting priorities, delegating responsibility, and, when needed, asking for help. Personal peace can be achieved when, despite all other demands, we say yes to Jesus first.

World Peace Starts at Home

"Give me that!"

"No, it's mine!"

"NOOO, it's mine! Dad said I could have it!"

"Mom said we have to share! You need to share with me."

"No! Give it back!"

Sound familiar? The sweet sounds of "Mom, Morgan hit me!" and "Mom, Peyton took my favorite toy!" echo through my home on an all-too-regular basis. I remember getting into fights with my own sister; these arguments and brawls seem to be part of growing up. And though I hate to deal with them, they are very teachable moments. It sounds Pollyannish, but I believe world peace starts at home. Selfishness, anger and pride—all are enemies of peace.

When I teach my children to share, to solve their problems without letting them escalate, and I show them how to respect each other, I am teaching them peacemaking skills they can use in all of life.

Peace starts one person at a time. So many families don't seem to know how to get along. Family feuds have been around longer than Richard Dawson—and why? Because many of us don't know how to (1) overlook our own interests, (2) negotiate compromise, and (3) forgive grievances. Grudges spoil the soil surrounding the family tree, leaving everyone thinking that only rotten apples are growing.

This is not God's heart for us. He offers so much more. But how can we get along with colleagues or others of a different political affiliation—not to mention from other countries—when we can't agree to disagree with the people under our own roof? Changing our hearts, tapping into the peace that transcends all understanding (see Philippians 4:7) on a personal level, creating margin, and teaching our children acceptance, compromise and a loving coexistence are all steps toward the peace God wants for us.

A Cup of Peace

Peace is not simply the absence of turmoil or chaos; deep peace exists in these situations when we acknowledge Jesus as the Calm in the chaos. He quells our nervousness when life has us feeling like a fizzy soda; He turns down the volume when the sub-woofer of our schedule shakes our foundation. He shows us the composure in every trial. "The fruit of righteousness will be peace; the effect of righteousness will be quietness and confidence *forever*" (Isaiah 32:17, emphasis added).

"Women are brought into freedom and into the walk in the Spirit in the same way men are: by listening to God and doing what they hear Him say." —LEANNE PAYNE, *THE HEALING PRESENCE*[3]

John Lennon once said, "Give peace a chance." Pope John Paul II said, "Teach peace." Psalm 34:14 and 1 Peter 3:11 tell us to "Seek peace and pursue it." I say: Don't give up. Peace is there for you, even when it doesn't seem like it. When the coffee is spilling, the children are feuding and your schedule implodes, look to Jesus. When the kids scream, when you lose a dream and when the money runs out, look to Jesus. In every situation look to Him and let God's peace radiate warmth throughout your soul, melting chaos and troubles into a sea of tranquility.

Questions to STIR

1. Do you have peace and margin in your daily life? If not, what steps can you take to create some breathing room?

2. Isaiah 53:5 says, "The punishment that brought us peace was upon him." How can you experience the fullness of God's gift of peace?

3. Read Hebrews 13:20-21. What kind of life might you experience when God's peace is realized in your life? What kind of life as a friend? A wife? A mom?

Soul Sip Solutions

1. The next time your child gets in an argument with a sibling or a schoolmate, use the opportunity to teach acceptance and compromise.

2. Are you at peace with all members of your family? Why or why not? If there are hard feelings from a prior conflict, take a step toward peace with your loved ones.

3. Take a moment to think about the importance of respecting others' beliefs and opinions. Jesus loved others, regardless of their skin color or political opinions. How can we be more accepting and tolerant of others who are different from us?

Reflection and Challenge

Think of a difficult circumstance that has happened to you. How can you look through the trial to find an opportunity to be more tolerant, accepting or forgiving? What do you think is meant by Robert Frost in his poem *Mending Wall* (1914) when he said, "Good fences make good neighbors"?

_____

_____

_____

_____

_____

_____

_____

_____

_____

_____

_____

_____

_____

_____

_____

_____

_____

_____

_____

_____

_____

_____

_____

COFFEE BREAK
WITH TERRI

Dear Moms,

If you want some peace, please stand in line. Everywhere I look someone wants a piece. I hear "Give me this" and "Can I have that?" "Take me here" and "You forgot . . ." In moments of chaos, I want to give a piece of my mind, but that will *not* bring peace.

It seems that when I look at my surroundings for peace I just find lack—

With five kids, I hear very little quiet, and no one ever has enough.

Peace doesn't come when everyone gets what he or she wants from me.

It comes from how I respond to what they want.

Peace is an internal thing, but it comes outside of the moment.

I feel peace when I look at the mess, hear the noise and think about something bigger and more lasting than order and quiet. *I know I will get those things just around the corner: Just blink and kids grow up and drive away.*

Peace comes when:

I love—my husband and my kids.

I do my best—to meet people where they are, not where I want them to be.

I listen—long enough to understand their perspective.

I realize—this is only a moment; it will soon be over and

I pray. Prayer affects everything else. It helps me be thankful for what I have as I understand that there is a bigger story and it connects me to a Source whom I can't quite explain, but I know *always* brings peace.

Peace to you!
Terri Powell

29

A PLEASING AROMA

Worship and Praise

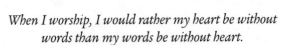

When I worship, I would rather my heart be without words than my words be without heart.
LAMAR BOSCHMAN

Worship the LORD with gladness; come before him with joyful songs.
PSALM 100:2

"We're late. We needed to leave earlier."

"We're not late," I reply. "They sing for at least 20 minutes before the service actually starts."

"No, the service starts at 9:00. We're late."

"Well, it's only 8:58 right now," I say as we turn into the church parking lot. We're not that late."

"Yes. We are," Pete says emphatically. "By the time we park, walk in, check-in the kids and get coffee, we will be 15 minutes late."

"It won't take us that long," I continue to argue. But by then it is time to stop the bickering and get moving. We help the girls out of the backseat and hightail it into church.

Fifteen minutes later, we are in the sanctuary. The worship band is leading the congregation in song. My husband immediately starts to sing, but I sip my coffee and look around. Some people stand with arms outstretched, singing with robust, heavenly vigor. Others sing quietly, eyes closed, gently swaying. Some sit, heads bowed in prayer. There are some like me, clutching lattes and looking around, and others just reading the words on the screen—going through the motions with no real engagement. A few read the bulletin.

> *Worship is not about us. Worship is about God.*

I put down my coffee and pray that God will help me get in the right mindset. But as soon as I begin to sing, the lady next to me takes it up an octave—or 10—singing like a Russian opera star. Every time I try to sing a note, her loud, shrill voice floods my ears. It is really bugging me. I try to refocus, but I am having a hard time not feeling irritated. I steal a quick glance. I haven't seen her before; maybe she is a visitor and doesn't know "our style" of worship.

I look up at the stage and watch the band. The drummer looks like he is having fun. *I want to learn to play the drums.* I look at the family in front of me. *It doesn't look like that kid brushed his hair today.* I look to the right and see a friend. I wave. She waves back. I look to the left. The lady two seats over from Pete has a really cute purse. *I bet she got that at Nordstrom.* I try to refocus on singing, but opera-girl is making me crazy. *I don't even recognize this song.* My stomach grumbles. *I'm kind of hungry. I wonder if it will be a long message today.* At last, the music ends and we bow our heads to pray. Phew! Finally, *now* I can focus on God.

Perspective in Worship

Worship is not about us. Worship is about God. Worship is honoring, adoring and praising the greatness of God; it is a posture of the heart. I admit that it can be easy to forget what worship is about. As highlighted in the story above, I used to think of this precious time to honor God as a buffer until the *real* service began. My thinking was way wrong. Worship is a time when we turn our attention from our stuff to God, a time when we humble ourselves and exalt our Creator. The sermon in a church service is generally a time when we receive God's Word, a time when God gives to us, but worship is a time *when we give to Him.*

So often, we fall into the trap of how worship makes us feel. If we like the songs or the instrumentals, we tend to think the worship service is good. And though the music is inspiring, it has little to do with the true heart of worship. My distracted thoughts and observations showed an inability to shut off the "self-talk" and turn to God. Perhaps, if I had arrived on time—or even a few minutes before the service began, to pray and prepare—my heart would have been in the right place. Walking in late left me disconnected and distracted, unable to bow to my King. Opera-girl, though irritating, was going for it. She was giving her all to God. Bless her. I was wrong to judge—or to put a box around any style of worship or praise. There will always be distractions—so just go for it. God is blessed by worship in whatever form, whether whispered in prayer or sung aloud— as long as our hearts are fully surrendered to Jesus.

Worship is not something we just do on Sundays or when we are at church. It is something we should aspire to every day. It is easy to think a devout life consists only of reading the Bible and praying, but that thought process is akin to thinking you make chocolate-chip cookies simply by stirring together flour, sugar and eggs. The sweet candy morsels are as integral to the cookies as worship is to our devotional life.

My worship pastor, Greg Russell, calls worship "critical" to personal devotions. He says, "I spend several hours in worship and prayer once a week (with shorter times in between), and it is the time where I get re-centered. Worship puts everything into perspective. We place such a high value on experience; we forget the scope of eternity. Worship is impossible without humility, so it also helps us keep our pride in check. Often when I worship, I sing scriptural truths that realign my priorities and let me see life from God's perspective."

Praise Personified

Praise is joyful and celebratory, glorifying God and acknowledging His essence; it is expressing thankfulness for His indwelling Spirit, and gratitude for His blessings. Hebrews 13:15 tells us to "continually offer to God a sacrifice of praise." We praise God in many ways. We praise God with words and with song. We praise God with good deeds and sharing Jesus with others; righteous living is praise without speaking. It is an "actions speak louder than words" motto on a grand scale. We praise God by our obedience, following His example, humbling ourselves, and giving God credit for being God—knowing that every good and perfect gift comes from Him (see James 1:17).

Last Christmas, Peyton, then eight, received a praise CD. She loves music, and after the holiday, we began to hear her with CD blaring, singing songs to Jesus in her room. One day, I was downstairs working in my office, particularly aware of her tender voice, each note threading together in perfect song. Her sweet song was blessing my heart—so I quietly climbed the stairs to peek at her, like a teenager creeping in after curfew. When I looked in, she was not only singing, but she was also tidying her room! I watched for a while as she made her bed and put her shoes away. Then three-year-old Morgan walked in through the Jack-and-Jill bath. She surveyed the room, looked at Peyton, then picked up Peyton's American Doll, a prized possession, and began to play.

I watched, waiting for war to break out. It didn't. Peyton looked at her sister, smiled and kept on cleaning, letting her little sister play with her favorite toy. No protest. No objections. No warnings. Just a smile that said: "It's okay. Go ahead."

"Come, let us bow down in worship, let us kneel before the Lord our Maker; for he is our God and we are the people of his pasture, the flock under his care." —PSALM 95:6-7

Peyton was praising God, but she was living it too. She was being obedient in cleaning her room and showing kindness to her sister, unselfish and gentle. Her simple example that day reminded me that our praise is empty if our lives don't back up our words.

A Cup of Worship and Praise

According to Don Williams in his book *Start Here: Kingdom Essentials for Christians*, "Worship, at its heart, is submission and surrender to the living God."[1] It's adoration and recognizing God's greatness. Praise is the outward expression, the song of our heart. Though we may read a psalm and be reminded, go to church and enter into song, and pray, the ultimate praise is a life that honors God *at all times*. A life lived seeking Him, being obedient, kind, patient, thankful and joyful is the essence of our worship and praise—the cake we bake Him: the frosting of praise on the worship cake of reverence. We honor God with the sweetness of both our worship and our praise.

The Bible is full of references reminding us of God's greatness and worth: "The LORD is my strength and my song; he has become my salvation. He is my God, and I will praise him" (Exodus 15:2). "The LORD lives! Praise be to my Rock!" (2 Samuel 22:47). "For great is the LORD and most worthy of praise" (1 Chronicles 16:25). "Let us continually offer to God a sacrifice of praise" (Hebrews 13:15).

Look to God in every moment, bow to Him, sing to Him—and live your life in a way that honors Him with worship and praise. Come on, girls, do I hear an *Amen* to that?

Questions to STIR

1. Psalm 95:6 says, "Come, let us bow down in worship, let us kneel before the Lord our Maker." When you worship and pray, do you have a practice of bowing or kneeling to signify humility before the Lord? How can the posture of your body communicate the posture of your heart?

2. Do you let your "stuff" interfere with truly worshiping God? How can you silence the distractions?

3. Read Romans 12:1. What does it mean to offer your body as a living sacrifice to God? What changes might need to take place?

Soul Sip Solutions

1. Most of the book of Psalms contains the songs of David's heart, expressing praise to God. Read a psalm every day this month and see if you find expressions to your vocabulary of praise.

2. Load your iPod with worship songs. Start to include a short time of worship and praise in your devotional time, singing to God.

3. Think of one way you can "live" an act of praise. Is it forgiving someone? Helping a person in need? Do it this week.

Reflection and Challenge

Write a psalm of praise to God, thanking Him for the blessings and love He's given you.

_____
_____
_____
_____
_____
_____
_____
_____
_____
_____
_____
_____
_____
_____
_____
_____
_____
_____
_____
_____

30

FULL TO THE BRIM

Life

Know this love that surpasses knowledge—that you may be filled
to the measure of the fullness of God.
EPHESIANS 3:19

I have come that they may have life, and have it to the full.
JOHN 10:10

We planned an impromptu family vacation to visit Pete's sister and family in McKinney, Texas, outside of Dallas. Pete and the girls wanted to leave earlier in the week, but I had a prior commitment, so I planned to follow them two days later. Pete booked the airline reservations.

"Well," he said, hanging up the phone, "I was able to get you a ticket, but for some reason, couldn't get you a seat assignment. They said you'll have to get one when you check in."

"Okay," I said, not thinking much of it.

Pete, Peyton and Morgan flew out on a Thursday, and I was to follow on Saturday. When Saturday rolled around, I made it a priority to get to the airport early, skipping my morning coffee and devotional, promising myself I'd study on the plane and grab a latte as soon as I was through security. Though I arrived two hours before my flight, when I got to the ticket counter, they were unable to assign a seat.

"I'm sorry, for some reason we cannot give you a seat," said the lady. "You'll need to go to secondary screening."

"Okay," I said, a little bugged. I walked to the second line and waited. Twenty minutes later, I was finally at the counter.

"How weird," said the attendant, pulling up my information, "we can't give you a seat assignment; you'll have to get it at the gate."

"But I have frequent-flyer status," I argued. "Why can't I get a seat?"

"I have no idea," he replied. "The computer won't let me give you one."

So off I went, through security, past the coffee bar and straight to the gate; I didn't want to chance missing my flight for lack of a seat assignment; the coffee could wait.

When I got to the gate, the agent took my ticket and then said matter-of-factly, "I'll call you when I have a seat."

I was the last person on the plane. After everyone had boarded, I was issued the last one, a middle seat in the back. I was not happy, to say the least. When I squeezed into my seat, I looked at the ladies on each side of me. One was reading a book; the other wore big, black Jackie O sunglasses and had her head resting against the window. I relaxed into my seat as the plane started to taxi.

Time for your Bible study, said a little voice inside my head.

I don't feel like doing a devotional, I thought back.

You'll feel better if you do, the voice said again.

I looked around. Everyone was engaged in their own stuff, but I still didn't want to whip out my Bible in such a public setting.

I don't want people to think I'm a weirdo. I'll do it later.

Who cares what they think, said the voice. *Why don't you do it now while you have time? Are you ashamed?*

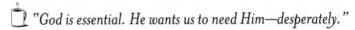 *"God is essential. He wants us to need Him—desperately."*

—John and Stasi Eldrege[1]

Aw, man. I wasn't ashamed, just nervous. After several more minutes of angel-devil banter, I decided that honoring God was more important than what others thought, so I pulled out my Bible and started to read.

The passage for the day spoke to my heart; I was deeply touched. I ended my devotional time in prayer, asking God to use me, however He might, to touch others for Jesus. Then when I started to tuck my Bible away, Jackie O looked up.

"Do you mind if I read your Bible?" she asked. "My mother died last night and I think it would bring me some comfort."

"Oh . . . sure," I said, shocked, handing her my small Bible.

She read for well over an hour, sniffing and quietly weeping.

As she read, my mind buzzed. No caffeine required. *When she gives you the Bible back, you should pray for her,* said the angel, who had reappeared on my shoulder. Praying for someone on a plane? This made reading the Bible a breeze. Praying out loud on an airplane, for someone I didn't know: This required a step of faith. But I knew I had to do it.

When Jackie O passed back the Bible, I struck up a conversation. Turns out, she lived just a few blocks from my church, and she, too, was headed to McKinney (where her mother had lived). She'd just purchased her ticket and received a last-minute seat assignment.

My mind swirled as the pieces of the puzzle came together.

"May I pray for you?" I asked, just as the drone of the jet engines sounded through the cabin.

"Please," she said.

As I prayed, she held my hand as if I were an old friend.

After the prayer, she said, "I thank God for you, because I know He put you next to me on this plane to bring me comfort."

Daily Courage

When I got off the plane, I could hardly believe how God had used me, knowing every detail, holding my seat assignment until Jackie O had hers. I thought how close I'd come to foiling the whole deal by not doing my devotional; if I hadn't pulled out my Bible, the interaction wouldn't have happened . . . and not only would I have lost out, but so would Jackie—sitting in sorrow alone.

It baffles me to think how many times God has probably wanted to use me, but pride, worry, fear and my agenda have frustrated the plan. You see, although the airplane story is pretty amazing, I have a whole closet full of stories where I didn't pull out my Bible. I have even more where I planned to—but then just got busy and forgot.

Consider when you are in need of one essential item at the grocery store. Let's say, for example, a loaf of bread. You get to the store and as you go down each aisle, you *remember* all the other stuff you *think* you need. So you load your cart until it is overflowing, and when you can't fit anything else into the buggy, you pay and head home. Then halfway home remember: "I forgot the bread!"

This is how many of us treat our spiritual lives. We intend to read our Bible and pray; we genuinely want to grow in faith. We want to be used by God in a powerful way, yet we let life distract us. Life pulls us, with stocked shelves of demand, obligation and expectation, and we load up, pushing around heavy carts full of stuff, overlooking the one thing that would give our whole trip purpose: the Bread of Life (see John 6:35).

Let God fill your cup to overflowing by making Him the first priority in your life. Seek Him and have the courage to step out in faith toward the life He has for you. It's scary; I'll admit it. Nobody wants to be viewed as different, but the reality is that followers of Jesus are different. The Bible says we are set apart (see Leviticus 20:26). Through Jesus, we are made whole and holy. We are forgiven our failures and there is grace for us, but grace is not a license for apathy. Take a close look at your life: Where do you get your strength? To whom are you looking for approval and acceptance? If it is anyone or anything other than God, you will never find it. "Am I now trying to win the approval of men, or of God? . . . If I were still trying to please men, I would not be a servant of Christ" (Galatians 1:10).

A Challenge for All

Anne Lamott, one of my favorite writers, says in her book *Traveling Mercies* that "a basic tenant of the Christian faith is that death is really just a major change of address."[2] This is a reason to celebrate! As followers of Jesus, we have the hope of eternal life with God after death. However, many of us use this truth like Linus with his security blanket. It makes us feel safe, no matter what happens in this life. But you know what? I once heard Todd Hunter, former President of the National Association of Vineyard churches, make this point: "Our favorite shorthand version of the gospel is: 'Say this prayer *so that* when you die you can go to heaven.' Think about it, what is this if not an open enticement to omit Jesus from our actual lives? Inadvertently we end up giving people a religion for death—not for life now."

Hello! This was a total wake-up call for me, catapulting me from my inconsistent devotionals and mediocre spiritual life. The power that raised Jesus from the dead is available to us now. Transformation is possible today. We can rise up into the fullness of God, who created us, and shine like stars in the universe (see Matthew 5:16). We can raise our children to know God and love Him. We can do it, for God is with us. God is our strength (see Psalm 46:1).

"Living fully in the present starts deep inside as we allow the self-protective shell to break open so the liberating grace of God can flow in to heal and renew and establish genuine meaning in our lives."

—LUCI SWINDOLL
I MARRIED ADVENTURE: LOOKING AT LIFE THROUGH THE LENS OF POSSIBILITY[3]

A Cup of Life

We moms have the potential to positively influence countless lives for God, especially our children's lives.

With our own lives on track, setting priorities and living fully in the power of Jesus, we can love others with all we are and share our awesome God. Whether you are an artist, a chef, an attorney, a nurse or whatever, God can use you. He's smart like that. Be open to possibility and yielded to Him.

Our most sacred responsibility and privilege is to nurture our children and help them know God's love. Be the hands of Jesus. Hug them. Listen to them. Give them an example of prayer. And be there. "Train a child in the way he should go, and when he is old he will not turn from it" (Proverbs 22:6).

Women who follow Jesus are the strongest women I know: courageous, fighting the Good Fight, believing in Truth, drawing on God and standing for what they believe. These women don't put their value in the world's currency; they know that accomplishment, financial success, popularity, material possessions—and yes, even coffee—can never give us a full cup. It all will fail. Only Jesus can fill our life cup to overflowing with blessings and abundance. "I have come that [you] may have life, and have it to the full" (John 10:10). That's God's promise—and much better than any extra large, quadruple shot, super foam, nonfat mochaccino will ever be.

Questions to STIR

1. Have you realized the full power of God in your life? In which areas do you still need to surrender to Him? What might be holding you back?

2. Where might you still be looking to the world for affirmation and value (i.e., appearance, financial status or your role as a mother)? How can you change your paradigm, looking to God instead?

3. Do you truly believe God can transform you? Where might you doubt? Pray for courage to lean in to Jesus.

Soul Sip Solutions

1. Take a walk and thank God for His goodness. Breathe deeply and envision your life cup overflowing with blessing.

2. Flip back through the book to any chapters that had special application in your life. Complete a previous "Soul Sip Solution" you meant to do but didn't.

3. Pray for your children. Ask God to guide you as a mom. Ask God to continue to reveal Himself to your family in powerful ways. Continue to seek Him. You will be blessed.

Reflection and Challenge

In your journey through this book, if you have experienced Jesus in significant ways but have never made a decision to commit your life to Him—or if you'd like to recommit your life to Jesus—you can do so by praying the prayer below. These are not magic words; there is no secret mantra or script. Coming to Jesus begins with a posture of the heart—surrendering to Him and asking for forgiveness. If these words feel awkward, speak from your own heart—and just use this prayer as a guide.

> *Dear Jesus, My cup is empty. It is empty because of a lack of faith and hope in You. I want to turn from my old ways and start anew. Please forgive me and come into my life. Help me follow You as my Savior. And may my cup overflow with trust, love, joy and eternal life. Thank You, Jesus. Amen.*

If you prayed this prayer, congratulations! I encourage you to make a note of it in this book and in your Bible. Date it. Tell a church leader or trusted friend about your decision. If you are not involved in a local church, seek the support and friendship of other followers of Jesus to encourage you in your faith.

Here are some additional verses to look up and study: John 3:16; Romans 10:9; Romans 3:23-24; Revelation 3:20. Journal any thoughts about those verses.

_____

_____

_____

_____

_____

_____

_____

_____

CONCLUSION

The only values you pass on are the ones you live.
LINDA TITCOMB

You anoint my head with oil; my cup overflows. Surely goodness and love will follow me all the days of my life, and I will dwell in the house of the LORD forever.
PSALM 23:5-6

"What do you do to fill up?" my friend Tonya asked not long ago. "You give out so much, what refills you?"

Well, I thought, *God fills me: my cup, my pitcher, my tank. He, alone, provides all I need: grace, forgiveness, hope, joy, love . . . the list goes on. Walking with God and trusting Him completely, I am a better person, a more patient mom, sharing joy, loving well, living fully.*

And yet . . .

And yet, I don't always live there. There are days when I feel too tired to drag my sorry self out of bed for devotional time, coffee or no coffee. Some days I over-schedule myself and don't take the time. It's at these times that I'm an apathetic child in life's scavenger hunt—too fatigued to look for all God has promised (most of it in plain sight). Can you relate? This is not the life we are meant to live. Not even close.

The fact is, the world pulls us in a bazillion directions, and just as dinner does not make itself, spiritual growth does not just happen. It takes consistent effort. Even then, life may bring challenges that put our beliefs to the test. I am so grateful that God is patient and merciful, loving and forgiving, or the reality is that I'd have been voted off faith island long ago.

In the midst of writing this book, Peyton had a follow-up MRI that revealed what may be slow tumor regrowth in her brain. Instantly, I was faced with an internal interrogation: *Can you live it? Can you walk the talk and believe, despite what the tests say, that God loves*

*you, loves Peyton and that all things truly work together for the good of those
who love Him? Or are you going to let doubt creep in? Will you still believe
in His goodness if her tumor continues to grow?*

I still believe. Always will. If I know anything, it is that God is
great and good, and my finite brain cannot even come close to
grasping the big picture of why and how it all fits together. I know
He loves me, my daughters, my husband, all of us. He loves us so
much that He died for us. And because of that, I am confident of
hope (and life!) beyond this life; I have hope not only for tomorrow
but for today.

Jesus gives me the power to change the way I live now. I can with-
stand the storms because He's got me. I don't have to live an angry,
anxious existence. The Holy Spirit fills my cup to *overflowing*. I can
be patient, kind, loving, compassionate, joyous. Faith in God's goodness means that I can be a fantastic mom, savoring every moment.

You can too.

God has brought many wonderful "moms" into my life who
have nurtured, mentored and encouraged me in my faith, my parenting and in living a full, purposeful life. (Some of them have written the Coffee Break letters.) My prayer is that God will bring
"mom" connections and unexpected surprises of support into your
life as well, whereby you are blessed and your cup overflows to others, especially to your children.

God is reaching out His hand. We, like Peter, need to simply
reach out to Him (see Matthew 14:28-31). Draw near to Him and
He will draw near to you (see James 4:8). Give your heart to God
and enter into the full life you are meant to live. Let Him restore
you. Let Him pour into you and fill your cup. My friend, there is
nothing on this earth that will ever come close.

*I pray that you, being rooted and established in love,
may have power, together with all the saints, to grasp how wide
and long and high and deep is the love of Christ, and to know this
love that surpasses knowledge—that you may be filled to
the measure of all the fullness of God.*
EPHESIANS 3:17-19

ENDNOTES

Chapter 1: Thirsty (Affirmation)

1. "Specialty Coffee Statistics and Coffee Facts," E-Imports, March 6, 2007, http://www.e-importz.com/Support/specialty_coffee.htm (accessed January 2008).

2. Jared Jost, "What Is a Mom Worth? Working Mom vs. Stay At Home Mom Salaries for 2006," Salary.Com, Inc., May 3, 2006. www.salary.com/aboutus/layoutscripts/abtl_default.asp?tab=abt&cat=cat012&ser=ser041&part=Par481 (accessed January 2008).

Chapter 2: The Daily Grind (Rest)

1. "Specialty Coffee Statistics and Coffee Facts," E-Imports, March 6, 2007, http://www.e-importz.com/Support/specialty_coffee.htm (accessed January 2008).

2. Cheryl Richardson, "Inner Growth: Tired but Wired," *Body and Soul*, March 2006.

3. Rick Warren, *The Purpose Driven Life* (Grand Rapids, MI: Zondervan Publishing, 2002), p. 177.

Chapter 3: Latte Letdown (Grace)

1. "From My Home to Yours: Barista Basics," *Martha Stewart Living Magazine*, January 2008, p. 24.

2. Anne Lamott, *Traveling Mercies* (New York: Pantheon Books, 1999), p. 142.

Chapter 4: A True Brew (Courage)

1. Helen Exley, *Wisdom for the New Millennium* (Hallmark Books, 1999).

2. C. S. Lewis, *The Horse and His Boy* (New York: HarperCollins, 1954), p. 164.

Chapter 5: A Fine Blend (Friendship)

1. "Socializing for Success," *Ladies' Home Journal*, February 2008, p. 14.

Chapter 6: A Shot of Laughter (Humor)

1. "Smile When You Say That!" *AARP*, May & June 2007.

Chapter 7: All Whipped Up (Support)

1. Linda Marsa, "Have You Gone Caffeine Crazy?" *Ladies' Home Journal*. June 2007, p. 148.

2. "I-35W Mississippi River Bridge," Wikimedia Foundation, Inc, 2008, http://en.wikipedia.org/wiki/I-35W_Mississippi_River_Bridge (accessed January 2008).

3. Judith Warner, *Perfect Madness: Motherhood in the Age of Anxiety* (New York: Riverhead Books, 2006), p. 217.

Chapter 9: What Did *She* Order? (Satisfaction)

1. Julie Rose, "Brain Power: Stop Looking at Me!" *Wondertime*. February 2008, p. 32.

Chapter 10: A Cup of Silence (Solitude)

1. Madeleine L'Engle, *Walking on Water: Reflections on Faith and Art* (Colorado Springs, CO: Waterbrook Press, 2001), p. 2.

2. Sarah Ban Breathnach, *Simple Abundance: A Daybook of Comfort and Joy* (New York: Warner Books, 1995), January 17.

3. Henry T. Blackaby and Claude V. King, *Experiencing God: Knowing and Doing the Will of God* (Nashville, TN: LifeWay Press, 1990), p. 81.

4. Luci Swindoll, *I Married Adventure: Looking at Life Through the Lens of Possibility* (W Publishing Group, 2002), p. 122.

Chapter 11: Your Own Special Blend (Purpose)

1. Loretta LaRoche, *Life Is Short—Wear Your Party Pants* (Carlsbad, CA: Hay House, Inc., 2003).

Chapter 12: "Extra Foam, Please" (Wonder)

1. Suzanne Rust, *Real Simple,* December 2007, p. 10.

   2. *Webster's Encyclopedic Unabridged Dictionary of the English Language* (New York: Random House Value Publishing, 2001), s.v. "wonder."

Chapter 13: Personalized Concoctions (Inspiration and Creativity)
   1. Quoted in "Thoughts," *Real Simple,* January 2008, p. 6.
   2. Julia Cameron, *The Artist's Way* (New York: G.P. Putnam's Sons, 1992), p. 194.
   3. Erik German, "Troops Find Safety in Silly String," *The Veterans Today Network,* December 8, 2006, www.veteranstoday.com/modules.php?name=News&file=article&sid=1780 (accessed January 2008).
   4. Helen Exley, *Wisdom for the New Millennium* (Hallmark Books, 1999).

Chapter 14: An Essential Ingredient (Respect)
   1. Linda Marsa, "Have You Gone Caffeine Crazy?" *Ladies' Home Journal,* June 2007, p. 150.
   2. Nanette Gartrell, M. D., "The Joys of Saying No," *Ladies' Home Journal,* February 2008, p. 19.

Chapter 15: Coffee and Donuts (Health and Wellness)
   1. "Specialty Coffee Statistics and Coffee Facts," E-Imports, March 6, 2007, http://www.e-importz.com/Support/specialty_coffee.htm (accessed January 2008).

Chapter 16: Keeping It Fresh (Courtship and Marriage)
   1. David H. Lowenherz, *The 50 Greatest Love Letters of All Time* (New York: Crown Publishers, 2002), p. 119.
   2. Stormie Omartian, *The Power of a Praying Wife* (Eugene, OR: Harvest House Publishers, 1997), p. 19.

Chapter 17: Will That Be a Small or a Tall? (Financial Savvy)
   1. "Happiness Flash," *Self,* December 2007, p. 130.
   2. Adapted from material originally published: Celeste Palermo, "The Experiment," *Today's Christian Woman,* Sept./Oct. 2007, pp. 36-37.

Chapter 19: A Sip at Sunrise (Consistency and Resolve)
   1. "The Two Sources of Cholesterol," American Heart Association, Inc., www.americanheart.org/presenter.jhtml?identifier=3046105 (accessed January 2008).

Chapter 24: Heavenly Brew (Hope)
   1. "Coffee Factoids, Stories, and Trivia," The Gourmet Coffee Club, www.gourmetcoffeeclub.com/cof_facts.htm (accessed January 2008).
   2. *Webster's Encyclopedic Unabridged Dictionary of the English Language* (New York: Random House Value Publishing, 2001), s.v. "hope."

Chapter 25: This Came from a Bean? (Faith)
   1. "Coffee Factoids, Stories, and Trivia," The Gourmet Coffee Club, www.gourmetcoffeeclub.com/cof_facts.htm (accessed January 2008).

Chapter 28: Security Smoothie (Peace)
   1. Nicky Gumbel, *Questions of Life* (Colorado Springs, CO: Cook Communications Ministries, 2003).
   2. Richard Swenson, *Margin* (Colorado Springs, CO: NavPress, 1992), p. 92.
   3. Leanne Payne, *The Healing Presence* (Grand Rapids, MI: Baker Books, 2005), p. 65.

Chapter 29: A Pleasing Aroma (Worship and Praise)
   1. Don Williams, *Start Here: Kingdom Essentials For Christians* (Ventura, CA: Regal Books, 2006), p. 230.

Chapter 30: Full to the Brim (Life)
   1. John Eldredge and Stasi Eldredge, *Captivating: Unveiling the Mystery of a Woman's Soul* (Nashville, TN: Nelson Books, 2005), p. 33.
   2. Anne Lamott, *Traveling Mercies* (New York: Pantheon Books, 1999), p. 63.
   3. Luci Swindoll, *I Married Adventure: Looking at Life Through the Lens of Possibility* (Nashville, TN: W Publishing Group, 2002), p. 57.

CONTRIBUTORS

Tamy Elam is a wife and home-school mom of four children: J. J., Jordan, Julianna and Joshua. She loves prayer, leading women in Bible study, laughter, reading great books and travel.

Susan Holloran is the mother of two grown boys and the author of two children's books: *Grandma Carrie's Sandwiches* and *The Pickle Man: Dreaming of the Majors*. She loves brisk morning walks, time spent with family, and sipping soy chai lattes on her front porch.

Mary Beth Lagerborg is a writer and speaker who served as publishing manager for MOPS International, helping to craft more than 70 books for moms. She is coauthor of the bestselling *Once-a-Month Cooking*, and her latest book is *Dwelling: Living Fully from the Space You Call Home*. She lives in Littleton, Colorado, with her husband, Alex. They have three grown sons. Visit her online at dwellingspace.com.

Joy Lehman has been a mom and stepmom for more than 26 years. She and her husband, Ric, are currently living in Puerto Vallarta, where they are pastoring an international English-speaking church and working with their nonprofit in the poor communities around the city. Her daughters, Abby, 27, and Bekah, 24, live in the States, and their son, Tucker, 18, is with them in Mexico.

Jane Norton is a mother of two grown children and stepmother to two grown children and six step-grandchildren. She is the former lieutenant governor of Colorado. She loves skinny chai lattes, skiing, hiking and serving in her church nursery with her husband, Mike.

Terri Powell is a wife and mother of five great children, ages 8 to 18. She works at an engineering firm and enjoys interacting with others and learning new things. Her days start with strong coffee with milk, and her favorite treat is a chai latte in the middle of the day.

Sarah Smiley is the mother of three young boys, Ford, Owen and Lindell, and the wife of a Navy pilot. When she's not writing her newspaper column "Shore Duty," which appears weekly in publications around the country, Sarah can be found laughing at the most inappropriate times.

Linda Titcomb has two daughters and four grandchildren. She is a retired nurse, an aspiring poet and a copilot for her husband, with whom she has coffee each morning.

Tandi Venter was born in Johannesburg, South Africa. She is a wife, mother of two boys, daughter, artist, musician, dreamer, wonderer and . . . of course, a princess. She starts every morning with a cup of tea. Her passion for music and culinary arts round out what is a truly expressive life.

Beth K. Vogt is the author of *Baby Changes Everything: Embracing and Preparing for Motherhood after 35*. She and her husband, Rob, are spread all over the parenting spectrum with children ages 24, 21, 19 and 7!

ABOUT THE AUTHOR

CELESTE PALERMO is the mother of two young daughters, and sharing her mothering journey and her faith is what gets her up in the morning (along with a double-shot vanilla latte!). She is the communications director for Smoky Hill Vineyard Church in Centennial, Colorado (where she lives with her husband, Pete), and the author of *From the Red Tees: Help, Hope, and Humor for the Women on the Green.* Celeste's work has appeared in *Chicken Soup for the Soul: A Tribute to Moms, Chicken Soup for the Woman Golfer's Soul, MomSense* magazine and *Today's Christian Woman.* Her life experiences include being a captain of the Denver Broncos Cheerleaders, taking a mission trip to tsunami-ravaged southern India, and completing 16 loads of laundry in one day. You can visit her online at www.celestepalermo.com.

MORE GREAT RESOURCES FROM
REGAL BOOKS

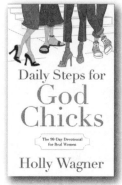